'Tis the
SEASON
a Vegetarian Christmas
Cookbook

Nanette Blanchard

ILLUSTRATIONS BY RODICA PRATTO
PHOTOGRAPHS BY SIMON METZ
DESIGNED BY BONNI LEON-BERMAN

SIMON & SCHUSTER
NEW YORK LONDON TORONTO SYDNEY TOKYO SINGAPORE

SIMON & SCHUSTER
Rockefeller Center
1230 Avenue of the Americas
New York, NY 10020
Copyright © 1995 by Nanette Blanchard
All rights reserved,
including the right of reproduction
in whole or in part in any form.
SIMON & SCHUSTER and colophon are registered trademarks
of Simon & Schuster Inc.

DESIGNED BY BONNI LEON-BERMAN

Manufactured in the United States of America
1   3   5   7   9   10   8   6   4   2

Library of Congress Cataloging-in-Publication Data
Blanchard, Nanette.
'Tis the season : a vegetarian Christmas cookbook / Nanette
Blanchard : illustrations by Rodica Pratto : photographs by Simon Metz.
p. cm.
Includes index.
1. Vegetarian cookery.   2. Christmas cookery.   3. Menus.
I. Title.
TX837.8554   1995
641.5′636—dc20   95-34166
CIP

ISBN 0-684-81155-3

Acknowledgments

First of all, I need to thank my husband, Bruce, for putting up with my manic Christmas preparations every year. I'm very grateful to my agent, Bill Adler, Jr., and my editor at Simon & Schuster, Sydny Weinberg Miner, for their help.

I'd like to thank all of the members on CompuServe's Cooks Online forum for their encouragement and inspiration. I especially want to express my appreciation to Michael Smith and John Yates for proofreading several of the chapters.

This book wouldn't be any good without the work of my recipe testers. Maureen Engeleit in New Jersey and Shelley Somerville in Vancouver tested the most recipes and I really appreciate all their hard work and suggestions. I'd also like to thank Hugh Blair, Hansje Kalff, Jackie Silberg, Lon Hall, John Patterson, Colleen Hartley, Laura Morgan, Debra Goldentyer, Alice Smith, Susan Haffey, and Bruce Sallee.

And finally, I'd like to thank Pumpkin, Sage, Bosco, and Friendly for making sure I was never alone in the kitchen while creating recipes.

Contents

Introduction

I was so excited at the idea of writing this book because I've always been crazy about holidays. I love everything about Christmas and I start planning the holiday months in advance.

I guess my fondness for celebrating holidays is genetic. My father actually telephoned me last year to wish me a happy Bastille Day and read me the introduction to *A Tale of Two Cities*. My mother sends prettily wrapped gifts to my cats and my brother faxes me birthday cards.

To me, Christmas is much more than just a day. It is a season for entertaining and celebrating and cooking. Christmas is a time for letting family and friends know how much I care about them. Cooking and hosting parties is the best way I know how to do this.

Because I don't like having people in the kitchen with me while I'm cooking, I really try to have as much work done as possible in advance of a dinner party. I also try to do parties where the guests do not have to do any of the work. This requires some planning but is well worth the extra effort. I hope the menus and recipes in this book can help you do advance planning for your next holiday bash.

A note about the ingredients: Some of the recipes in this book are high in fat, especially some of the desserts. I've tried to make sure the recipes in this book are balanced; some low-fat and healthful and some lavish desserts for special meals. Christmas happens only once a year and it just wouldn't be the same for me without the *bûche de noël*, the *croquembouche*, and the piles of brightly decorated cookies.

However, a dinner party can still be delicious without excess fat or dairy products, so I've tried to include a selection of recipes for vegans. I hope everyone will find menus that are right for them in this book.

Merry Christmas!

Make-Ahead Advent DINNER

Spinach-Cucumber Salad with Honey Vinaigrette

Sour Cream-Poppy Seed Loaf

Hearty Winter Stew

Winter Squash Cooked in Tomato Sauce

The Ultimate Lemon Bars

Cranberry-Cider Punch

This simple Advent menu can be made in advance and will serve approximately six people. I really like doing as much in advance as possible before a meal. It is so relaxing to be able to greet your guests or talk to your family without any last-minute cooking chores or worries. This make-ahead menu is intended to allow for a simple evening of reflection and anticipation of the holiday ahead.

Consider making an Advent wreath this year. All you need is a simple evergreen wreath in the center of the table with four white or lavender candles. The first Sunday of Advent my husband, Bruce, and I always try to have a simple dinner. We light the first of the four Advent candles and reflect on the season ahead. On each of the following Sundays, an additional candle is lit in the wreath in preparation for Christmas.

ALL ABOUT WREATHS

1. Bread dough makes a beautiful wreath. Braid a long strand of your favorite bread dough and attach both ends. Add a pretty ribbon at the top and you have a beautiful, edible gift.

2. Gather a few small branches or twigs and hang them upside down in a window. Decorate with glittery tinsel and a few tiny ornaments.

3. One of my favorite wreaths is a mixture of corn husks, small dried corncobs, and a variety of sizes and colors of dried chile peppers.

4. If you like wreaths, don't just limit yourself to hanging them on doors and windows! Put one on your refrigerator, on the hallway mirror, even on the front fender of your car. Use a wreath in the center of your dining room table adorned with your favorite tree ornaments. Or place a single red candle surrounded by a mound of peppermint candies in the center of an evergreen wreath.

5. String dried apple slices and form a circle for a simple, rustic wreath.

6. Hang a small round stained glass ornament in the center of an evergreen wreath in a window.

7. Use small fruits and vegetables for a natural wreath; try kumquats, cranberries, sun-dried tomatoes, chile peppers, crab apples, or whole walnuts or almonds.

Spinach-Cucumber Salad

Serves 6 to 8

1 POUND SPINACH, RINSED WELL AND COARSELY CHOPPED

4 CUCUMBERS, PEELED AND SLICED

1 SMALL RED ONION, THINLY SLICED

This refreshing salad can be prepared in advance. Make the Honey Vinaigrette (recipe follows) and serve it separately in an attractive cruet at the table. The dressing is also nice served with a salad of fresh fruit and greens.

Toss together all the ingredients in a serving bowl. Cover and refrigerate until serving time.

Honey Vinaigrette

Makes 1 cup

½ CUP APPLE CIDER VINEGAR

3 TABLESPOONS HONEY

½ TEASPOON DRY MUSTARD

½ TEASPOON SALT

½ CUP EXTRA-VIRGIN OLIVE OIL

In a small bowl, whisk together the vinegar, honey, mustard, and salt. Slowly add the oil in a stream, whisking continuously, until the dressing is slightly thickened.

Sour Cream–Poppy Seed Loaf

Makes 1 loaf

This beautiful loaf is delicious with a nice vegetable/pasta casserole like the one that follows. I use bread flour because this dough is rich with eggs, butter, and sour cream, which inhibit the gluten in the dough. The higher gluten content of bread flour helps the loaf rise better. Store poppy seeds in the refrigerator, since they can turn rancid at room temperature due to their high oil content. The bread freezes well.

1 TABLESPOON ACTIVE DRY YEAST
⅓ CUP WARM WATER (ABOUT 110 DEGREES)
2 TABLESPOONS SUGAR
1 TEASPOON SALT
¼ CUP UNSALTED BUTTER, MELTED AND COOLED
½ CUP SOUR CREAM, AT ROOM TEMPERATURE
1 EGG, AT ROOM TEMPER-ATURE
ABOUT 2½ CUPS BREAD FLOUR
1 EGG YOLK, FOR EGG WASH
2 TABLESPOONS POPPY SEEDS

In the bowl of an electric mixer, dissolve the yeast in the warm water for 10 minutes. Add the sugar, salt, butter, sour cream, and egg. Add the flour, 1 cup at a time. When the dough becomes thick, switch to dough hook. Continue adding the flour until the dough leaves sides of bowl. Knead for 8 minutes or until the dough is smooth and satiny.

Oil a bowl and turn the dough in the bowl to cover with oil. Cover with plastic wrap and let rise for 1½ hours or until doubled in bulk. Punch down the dough and let rest for 10 minutes. Divide the dough into 3 pieces and place each piece side by side in an 8½-by-3½-inch loaf pan sprayed with nonstick cooking spray. Let rise for 45 minutes or until almost doubled in bulk.

Preheat the oven to 375 degrees. Sprinkle the loaf evenly with poppy seeds. Bake for 30 minutes or until golden brown and the loaf sounds hollow when tapped on the bottom.

Hearty Winter Stew

Serves 6 to 8

1 MEDIUM ONION, DICED

2 TABLESPOONS OLIVE OIL

1 MEDIUM SWEET POTATO,
PEELED AND FINELY
CHOPPED

2 MEDIUM ZUCCHINI,
CHOPPED

4 CLOVES GARLIC, MINCED

1 TEASPOON SALT

2 (16-OUNCE) CANS GAR-
BANZO BEANS, RINSED
AND DRAINED

6 CUPS VEGETABLE BROTH

FRESHLY GROUND BLACK
PEPPER TO TASTE

1 (16-OUNCE) CAN YEL-
LOW HOMINY

½ TEASPOON DRIED BASIL

8 OUNCES ORZO PASTA,
UNCOOKED

This colorful main dish can be made in advance and reheated just before serving. If you can't locate canned yellow hominy, substitute 2 cups frozen corn kernels.

In a large Dutch oven, sauté the onion in the olive oil for 5 minutes over medium heat, stirring occasionally. Add the sweet potato and zucchini and continue cooking for another 5 minutes. Add the garlic and cook for an additional 3 minutes, stirring.

Add the salt, beans, broth, pepper, hominy, basil, and pasta and simmer for 20 minutes or until the orzo is tender.

Winter Squash Cooked in Tomato Sauce

Serves 4 to 6

This delicious dish is one of my favorite ways to serve squash. The flavor improves on standing, so try making this a day in advance.

3 CLOVES GARLIC, MINCED

2 TABLESPOONS EXTRA-VIRGIN OLIVE OIL

½ TEASPOON DRIED THYME

¼ TEASPOON CRUSHED RED PEPPER FLAKES

1 CUP TOMATO SAUCE

1½ POUNDS ACORN OR OTHER WINTER SQUASH, PEELED, SEEDED, AND CHOPPED (ABOUT 4 CUPS)

1 CUP WATER

8 KALAMATA OLIVES, PITTED AND SLICED

Sauté the garlic in the oil over medium heat for 2 minutes. Add the thyme and red pepper and sauté another 15 seconds or until fragrant. Add the tomato sauce and bring the mixture to a boil. Add the squash, water, and olives and cook for 30 minutes, uncovered, or until the squash is tender, stirring occasionally.

The Ultimate Lemon Bars

Makes 24 bars

2¼ CUPS UNBLEACHED
FLOUR, DIVIDED
1 CUP UNSALTED BUTTER
½ CUP CONFECTIONERS'
SUGAR PLUS ADDITIONAL
FOR DUSTING BARS
4 EGGS
2 CUPS SUGAR
¼ TEASPOON SALT
5 TABLESPOONS FRESH
LEMON JUICE
⅛ TEASPOON LEMON OIL
OR 1 TABLESPOON GRAT-
ED LEMON ZEST
1 TEASPOON BAKING POW-
DER

Believe it or not, I first tasted lemon bars only about a year ago at a local coffeehouse and was amazed at their wonderful buttery, lemony flavor. I use Boyajian's lemon oil, which is available through Williams-Sonoma or the King Arthur Flour Baker's Catalogue (see Mail-Order Sources, page 221). The lemon oil gives them a boost of fresh lemon flavor without tasting artificial. Lemons really vary in quality. Buy the best to give these lemon bars the strongest lemon flavor. Avoid largish lemons with a very thick pith; they often yield 2 tablespoons juice or less per lemon. Look for small, heavy lemons instead. These lemon bars always disappear fast at potlucks.

Preheat the oven to 350 degrees. With a pastry blender or fork, mix 2 cups of the flour, the butter, and the confectioners' sugar until crumbly. Pat the mixture into a 13-by-9-inch baking pan. Bake for 20 minutes or until just brown. Do *not* overbake.

With an electric mixer, beat the eggs, sugar, salt, lemon juice, lemon oil or zest, remaining ¼ cup flour, and baking powder until frothy. Pour into the hot crust. Bake for 25 minutes or until firm to the touch. Cool on a baking rack; cut into 2-inch squares. With a flour sifter, sprinkle the bars evenly with confectioners' sugar.

Cranberry-Cider Punch

Serves 8 to 12

This colorful and easy punch is decorated with an attractive ice ring.

1 QUART CRANBERRY
JUICE
1 QUART APPLE CIDER
1 CUP CRANBERRIES
2 ORANGES, HALVED AND
THINLY SLICED
2 CUPS FRESH ORANGE
JUICE

To make the punch, combine the cranberry juice and apple cider. Chill for at least 2 hours. To make the ice ring, mix the cranberries and oranges in a 4-cup mold. Add the orange juice and freeze for several hours or until firm. Pour the punch into a serving bowl and float the ice ring on top.

FOOD FOR KIDS

1. There are so many fun ways to fix up food for children. Buy some large lollipops and make faces on them with marshmallows and gumdrops. If the candy does not stick to the lollipops, moisten them slightly and press firmly. Another fun thing to decorate is pancakes—they are the perfect shape. Use dried fruits, berries, and nuts to make faces on your kids' pancakes.

2. Have your kids trace their hands onto cookie dough with the handle of a wooden spoon. Trim away the excess dough and decorate the cookies for a special gift for grandparents.

3. Make red and green gelatin in two shallow pans and cut out shapes with Christmas cookie cutters.

4. If you don't want to mess up your kitchen making Christmas cookies, cut out gingerbread men shapes from brown cardboard and decorate with crayons, paints, and felt-tip pens. These make terrific ornaments or gift tags.

5. Use cookie cutters to cut peanut butter and jelly sandwiches into Christmas tree, snowman, and Santa shapes. You can also do this with cheese slices.

6. For some truly edible art, fill a 9-by-13-inch baking dish with mashed potatoes. Then ask your kids to create a landscape using steamed-broccoli trees, red-pepper-strip mountains, mushroom-stem roads. If they decorate it, they're more likely to eat it!

7. Instead of making a three-dimensional gingerbread house, try making a one-dimensional house. Simply roll out gingerbread dough to a thickness of about ¼ inch on a cookie sheet and trace the outline of your house onto it with a knife. Bake and have the kids decorate it with store-bought colored frostings. It might help to have a photo of the front of your house when you do this.

A VICTORIAN CHRISTMAS Tea

 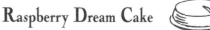

One of my favorite English traditions is the tea service. The nice thing about giving a tea is that it can be held in an informal setting, such as your living room or family room.

If you live in a warm climate, you can give a tea outside on your patio or deck. Most of the sweet and savory recipes in this menu can be made in advance.

Teas are a relaxing way to entertain, and guests always feel pampered when you bring out your best china and your finest teapot. They are a perfect way to entertain your bridge club, aerobics class, your neighbors, or even your family.

Children really enjoy learning how to serve and pour tea properly. You can heat up some cider or prepare an herb tea for the kids to drink out of the teacups. I often like to do a simplified version of this menu for my husband and myself on lazy Sunday afternoons while we read the paper and watch the sunset.

Crumpets

Makes about 16 crumpets

1 TABLESPOON ACTIVE DRY YEAST

¼ CUP WARM WATER (ABOUT 110 DEGREES)

3½ CUPS UNBLEACHED FLOUR

1¾ CUPS MILK, AT ROOM TEMPERATURE

2 TEASPOONS SALT

1 TEASPOON SUGAR

4 TABLESPOONS VEG-ETABLE OIL, DIVIDED

½ TEASPOON BAKING SODA

½ CUP WARM WATER (ABOUT 110 DEGREES)

This recipe, one of my favorites, is adapted from Elizabeth David's *English Bread and Yeast Cookery.* Most people believe that crumpets are like English muffins, but they are actually more like thick, dense pancakes. You'll need some type of rings to cook crumpets properly. I use egg rings, which are about 3 inches in diameter. Sweet Celebrations and other baking catalogs (see Mail-Order Sources, page 221) sell muffin rings for this purpose. You can also cut off both ends of similarly sized cans to make your own rings. Crumpets freeze well, but you can also make these the same day of the tea and reheat them in the microwave. The best way to serve them is dripping with plenty of honey and butter.

In the bowl of an electric mixer, dissolve the yeast in the ¼ cup warm water for 10 minutes. With a dough hook, mix in the flour, milk, salt, sugar, and 2 tablespoons of the oil and knead for 5 minutes. Cover the dough and let rest in a warm place for 30 minutes.

Mix the baking soda with the ½ cup warm water and add to the dough. Knead for another 10 minutes. Lightly spray the crumpet rings with nonstick cooking spray. Heat a cast-iron griddle (or 2 skillets) over medium-high heat and add the remaining 2 tablespoons oil. Put about ¼ cup batter in each crumpet ring on the hot griddle.

Cook until the batter puffs up and tiny bubbles appear on the tops of the crumpets. Carefully remove the rings and turn the crumpets. Continue cooking for 3 to 4 minutes or until the crumpets are lightly browned. Repeat with the remaining batter.

Easy Cinnamon Toast

Makes 24 rectangles

3 TABLESPOONS UNSALTED BUTTER

6 SLICES SANDWICH BREAD, TOASTED

2 TABLESPOONS SUGAR

1 TABLESPOON GROUND CINNAMON

You're probably wondering why you bought a book with a recipe for cinnamon toast, but do consider this recipe when you need a simple yet delicious tea sweet. I've included it at the suggestion of one of my British friends. I like to cut the toast into four rectangles, but you can also use cookie cutters.

You can use any type of sandwich bread, such as raisin bread, whole-wheat bread, and sourdough bread, for this recipe. Just make sure you don't burn the toast! It is probably best to stand right next to the oven with a hot pad in hand while broiling the bread slices.

Butter each slice of toast. In a small bowl, mix the sugar and cinnamon. Sprinkle the sugar mixture over the toast slices. Broil about 4 inches from the heat source for 30 seconds or until the sugar mixture just starts to sizzle. Cut each slice into 4 pieces.

Thyme Scones

Makes 16 scones

2 CUPS UNBLEACHED
FLOUR

1 TEASPOON SALT

1 TABLESPOON BAKING
POWDER

2 CLOVES GARLIC, MINCED

3 TABLESPOONS MINCED
FRESH THYME OR 1
TABLESPOON DRIED

1 CUP WHIPPING CREAM
PLUS ADDITIONAL FOR
BRUSHING SCONES

These tender, flaky scones are best served warm from the oven. For a prettier presentation, try cutting the scones out with holiday cookie cutters.

In a large bowl, mix together the flour, salt, and baking powder. Add the garlic, thyme, and cream and stir until a soft dough forms. Place the dough on a floured surface and knead 10 times or until it forms a ball.

Preheat the oven to 425 degrees. Divide the dough into 2 pieces. Pat each piece out to a 10-inch circle on an ungreased cookie sheet. Brush the top of the dough with cream. Bake for 15 minutes or until golden brown. Cut each circle into 8 wedges.

Sally's Baked Apple Pancake

Serves 8 as a first course

My mother-in-law operated a bed-and-breakfast called Farm Home in Fly Creek, New York. This wonderful pancake was her signature dish. For this menu, I like to cut the pancake into thin slices and serve it hot from the oven. Although a baked pancake is not traditional tea fare, this one is delicate enough to make the translation. This recipe also makes a light main dish for brunch or supper for four people.

2 TART APPLES, SUCH AS GRANNY SMITH

¼ CUP CONFECTIONERS' SUGAR PLUS ADDITIONAL FOR DUSTING PANCAKE

1 TEASPOON GROUND CINNAMON

1 TEASPOON FRESH LEMON JUICE

6 TABLESPOONS UNSALTED BUTTER, DIVIDED

4 EGGS, BEATEN

½ TEASPOON SALT

½ CUP MILK

½ CUP UNBLEACHED FLOUR

Preheat the oven to 400 degrees. Peel, core, and thinly slice the apples. Mix the apples with the confectioners' sugar, cinnamon, and lemon juice. Melt 4 tablespoons of the butter in an ovenproof skillet. Sauté the apple mixture over medium-high heat in the butter until just tender, about 4 to 5 minutes. Set aside. Melt the remaining 2 tablespoons butter. Whisk together the eggs, salt, milk, flour, and melted butter. Pour over the apple mixture and bake for 20 minutes or until puffy and slightly brown on top. Dust with confectioners' sugar. Cut into thin slices for serving. Serve hot.

Chocolate Crescents

Makes about 5 dozen pastries

Dough

½ CUP UNSALTED BUTTER, SOFTENED

1 (8-OUNCE) PACKAGE CREAM CHEESE, SOFT-ENED

1½ CUPS ALL-PURPOSE FLOUR

¼ TEASPOON SALT

Filling

1 (6-OUNCE) BAG MINIA-TURE SEMISWEET CHOCO-LATE CHIPS

¾ CUP FINELY CHOPPED WALNUTS

½ CUP SUGAR

1½ TEASPOONS GROUND CINNAMON

Topping

3 TABLESPOONS SUGAR

1 TEASPOON GROUND CIN-NAMON

These small pastries resemble croissants. The rich cream cheese dough is easy to work with but needs to be well chilled first. These freeze very well and can also be stored in an air-tight container for several days before serving.

To make the dough: With an electric mixer, cream the butter and cream cheese until well blended. Add the flour and salt to the cream cheese mixture and beat until smooth. Divide the dough into 4 pieces and roll into balls. Flatten the balls slightly, adding more flour if dough is still sticky. Wrap the dough in plastic wrap and chill several hours or overnight.

To make the filling: Mix together the chocolate chips, walnuts, sugar, and cinnamon in a small bowl.

To make the topping: Mix together the sugar and cinnamon in another bowl.

Preheat the oven to 350 degrees. Remove 1 ball of dough from the refrigerator. On a floured surface, roll out to a 12-inch circle. Sprinkle with one-quarter of the filling ingredients and lightly press the filling into the dough. Cut the dough circle into 16 pie-shaped wedges.

Starting at the outside edge, roll up each of the wedges croissant-style. Place the pastries on an ungreased baking sheet and sprinkle with the cinnamon sugar. Bake for 15 to 20 minutes or until light golden brown. Repeat this process with the remaining dough.

Remove from the oven and let cool on a rack.

Eggnog-Pineapple Bread

Makes 2 loaves

This moist bread is an interesting way to use commercial dairy eggnog. Like most quick breads, it tastes better the second day, so make it in advance. This recipe makes two loaves and is a nice holiday gift wrapped in plastic wrap and a big red ribbon. I use commercial dairy eggnog quite often. Try substituting it for the heavy cream in the Cheesecake with Caramelized Lemon Zest (page 152) or the Eggnog Ice Cream (page 177).

3¼ CUPS UNBLEACHED FLOUR
½ CUP SUGAR
4 TEASPOONS BAKING POWDER
½ TEASPOON SALT
½ TEASPOON FRESHLY GRATED NUTMEG
1 EGG
1¾ CUPS DAIRY EGGNOG
¼ CUP VEGETABLE OIL
1 (20-OUNCE) CAN UNDRAINED CRUSHED PINEAPPLE IN UNSWEETENED JUICE
1 CUP CHOPPED PECANS

Preheat the oven to 350 degrees. Spray two 8½-by-4½-inch loaf pans with nonstick cooking spray. In a large bowl, whisk together the flour, sugar, baking powder, salt, and nutmeg. In a separate bowl, mix the egg, eggnog, oil, and pineapple. Add the dry ingredients to the wet ingredients and stir just until mixed. Gently fold in the pecans.

Pour the batter into the prepared pans. Bake for 1 hour or until a toothpick inserted comes out clean. Cool the bread in the pans for 10 minutes, then remove and cool on a baking rack.

Cucumber-Cream Cheese Sandwiches

Makes 16 sandwich triangles

1 (8-OUNCE) PACKAGE
CREAM CHEESE, SOFT-
ENED
1 CLOVE GARLIC, CRUSHED
1 TABLESPOON FRESH
LEMON JUICE
1 SCALLION, FINELY DICED
1 TABLESPOON FINELY
CHOPPED ITALIAN PARS-
LEY
1 TABLESPOON MINCED
FRESH CHIVES
8 THIN SLICES WHOLE-
GRAIN SANDWICH BREAD
1 CUCUMBER, PEELED AND
THINLY SLICED

I think every tea menu should have at least one sandwich selection. I often add lemon juice to savory dishes containing cream cheese to add flavor. To soften cream cheese, unwrap and microwave on High for 30 seconds.

Mix the cream cheese with the garlic, lemon juice, scallion, parsley, and chives. Spread the cream cheese mixture on 4 slices of the bread and top each slice with the thinly sliced cucumber. Top with another slice of bread and cut diagonally in both directions to make triangular sandwich shapes.

Raspberry Dream Cake

Serves 12

This is my adaptation of a recipe I found in the first of Diane Mott Davidson's culinary mystery series, <u>Catering to Nobody</u>. It is a nice cross between a cake and a cheesecake.

I try to use seedless raspberry preserves for this cake, although they aren't necessary. It is better to make this cake ahead and refrigerate it, since it improves with standing.

Crust

2¼ CUPS ALL-PURPOSE FLOUR
¾ CUP SUGAR
¾ CUP UNSALTED BUTTER
1 EGG, BEATEN
¾ CUP SOUR CREAM
¼ TEASPOON SALT
½ TEASPOON BAKING POWDER
½ TEASPOON BAKING SODA
1 TEASPOON ALMOND EXTRACT

Filling

1 (8-OUNCE) PACKAGE CREAM CHEESE, SOFTENED
1 EGG, BEATEN
¼ CUP SUGAR
1 CUP RASPBERRY PRESERVES
⅓ CUP CHOPPED ALMONDS

Preheat the oven to 350 degrees. Spray a 9-inch springform pan with nonstick cooking spray.

To make the crust: Mix the flour and sugar together. With a pastry blender, add the butter to the flour mixture until small crumbs form. Reserve 1 cup of the crumb mixture. To the remaining crumb mixture, add the egg, sour cream, salt, baking powder, baking soda, and almond extract and mix well. Spread the batter over the bottom and up the sides of the prepared pan with a spatula.

To make the filling: With an electric mixer, beat the cream cheese with the egg and sugar. Spread this mixture over the batter in the pan.

On top of the cream cheese mixture, spread the raspberry preserves. Mix the almonds with the reserved crumb mixture and sprinkle over the preserves on the cake. Bake the cake for 45 to 55 minutes or until a toothpick comes out clean. Cool the cake for at least 30 minutes before serving.

A Proper Pot of Tea

Makes 1 pot of tea

I use a ceramic teapot with a built-in strainer insert. You can also use a mesh tea infuser or wait and strain the tea after it has brewed in the pot.

Bring cold water to a boil in a tea kettle. Carefully pour a small amount of the boiling water into a teapot to warm it. Swirl the water around, then drain. Use 1 teaspoon loose black tea per cup of water plus 1 teaspoon "for the pot." Pour the hot water over the tea. Let steep for 5 minutes before straining and serving.

Serve with lemon wedges, milk, and sugar or honey. The milk should be poured into the teacup before the tea.

NOTE: TRY STIRRING A TEASPOON OR SO OF ORANGE MARMALADE INTO YOUR TEACUP INSTEAD OF SUGAR OR HONEY.

Decorating with Candles

1. Votive candles are very inexpensive and fit in some imaginative containers, such as decorative molds, muffin tins, seashells, and upside-down clay flowerpots for a pretty glow. Put votives in hollowed-out apples, oranges, and winter squash for a nice scent. Make sure you level off the bottom of the fruit or vegetables first.

2. For a dripless evening, try putting all your candles in the refrigerator for at least 24 hours before you plan to burn them. Beeswax candles, although more expensive, won't drip. Be sure to buy enough candles for your party. If you have extra, use them to line your staircase or in the entryway or on the front porch to greet your guests. I always keep candles in my bathroom also so guests don't have to go groping around in the dark.

3. If you have a mirror or silver tray, try grouping a variety of white candles on it for an even prettier glow. Another way to get more sparkle from candles is to decorate them with gold and silver star stickers.

4. Homemade *farolitos* (often called *luminarias,* although *luminarias* are actually bonfires) are easy to make from brown paper lunch bags. Fold back the top of each bag about 2 inches and cut out several decorative designs (such as stars or snowflakes) in the bag. Fill with sand or cat litter and place a small votive candle (called the vigil candle) in the bag. Use the *farolitos* to line your driveway or the sidewalk up to your front door.

5. For an unusual serving dish, fill a basket or bowl with cookies, rolls, or pastries and anchor several long thin candles right in the center.

6. To personalize your candles, melt some candle wax (the easiest way to do this is to just burn a candle) and use it as an adhesive for herbs, dried flowers, and glitter. These homemade candles are also terrific gifts or party favors.

7. Any interesting piece of firewood can become an instant centerpiece if you drill a hole in the center large enough to fit a candle.

8. A pretty but simple Christmas centerpiece can be made easily by taking several large red candles of different heights and surrounding them with a ring of Granny Smith apples.

9. If you have children or pets, a nice way to safeguard burning candles is to place them in a bowl with 1 inch of water. Really shallow candles will even float in water.

Romantic
YULETIDE
CANDLELIGHT
Dinner

Creamy Potato-Leek Soup

Heart-Shaped Croutons

Marinated Yellow Bell Pepper and Zucchini Salad

Stuffed Acorn Squash

Microwave-Poached Vanilla Pears

Easy Strawberry Sauce

Sparkling Grape Goblets

It is really easy to forget the one you love the most during a holiday season when you're busy making cookies for the paperboy or fruitcake for your secretary. I like to serve romantic meals all through the year; I think that home-cooked food is probably one of the best ways of showing your love to your partner.

Turn down the lights, light all the candles you can find, throw a log on the fire, turn up the music, and toast each other with a Sparkling Grape Goblet. Christmas is the most romantic time of the year, so don't pass up an opportunity for a wonderful intimate evening together this Christmas season.

Creamy Potato-Leek Soup

Serves 2

1 LARGE LEEK, RINSED
  WELL AND THINLY SLICED
1 TABLESPOON UNSALTED
  BUTTER
4 YUKON GOLD POTATOES,
  PEELED AND CHOPPED
3 CUPS VEGETABLE BROTH
2 TABLESPOONS SOUR
  CREAM
SALT AND WHITE PEPPER
  TO TASTE.

This warm version of the classic vichyssoise is a delicious addition to any romantic menu. Decorated with Heart-Shaped Croutons (recipe follows) and served in some colorful earthenware bowls, this soup is sure to warm the heart. If you want to make the soup in advance, add the sour cream at serving time and reheat gently over low heat.

In Dutch oven over medium heat, sauté the sliced leek in the butter for 10 minutes or until soft. Add the potatoes and vegetable broth; cover and bring to a boil. Reduce the heat to medium and cook 20 to 30 minutes or until tender. Puree in a blender or food processor, stir in the sour cream, and season with salt and white pepper.

Heart-Shaped Croutons

Makes 6 croutons; Serves 2

These croutons can be made in advance and stored in a covered container in the refrigerator.

2 SLICES SOURDOUGH
SANDWICH BREAD
4 CLOVES GARLIC
1 TABLESPOON EXTRA-
VIRGIN OLIVE OIL

Toast the bread or let it sit out uncovered for a day or so to become stale. With a small heart-shaped cookie cutter, cut 3 hearts from each slice of bread. Smash the whole garlic cloves and place in a nonstick pan with the oil. Add the bread and cook, stirring occasionally, over medium heat, until golden on both sides. Discard the garlic.

Marinated Yellow Bell Pepper and Zucchini Salad

Serves 2

1 MEDIUM YELLOW BELL
PEPPER, SLICED
1 MEDIUM ZUCCHINI,
HALVED AND THINLY
SLICED
1 TABLESPOON EXTRA-
VIRGIN OLIVE OIL
1 TABLESPOON WHITE
WINE VINEGAR
½ TEASPOON GROUND
CAYENNE PEPPER
1½ TEASPOONS *GOMASIO*

This salad is at its best served at room temperature. Steaming the vegetables and adding the dressing while the vegetables are hot really improves the flavor in this salad. I buy gomasio (also spelled gomashio) at my health food store; it is a Japanese condiment that consists of equal parts toasted sesame seeds and salt. If you can't find gomasio, substitute ¾ teaspoon salt and ¾ teaspoon sesame seeds.

Steam the pepper and zucchini slices over boiling water for 5 minutes or until crisp-tender. Mix the oil, vinegar, cayenne, and *gomasio* and toss with the hot vegetables. Cover and chill at least an hour before serving. Bring to room temperature before serving.

Stuffed Acorn Squash

Serves 2

I really love winter squash. I buy a lot of it in fall and store it in a cool place to last me through the winter. There are two different types of acorn squash available today—the basic green type with orange flesh and a newer white type with a lighter yellow flesh. Acorn squash comes in many sizes; for this recipe look for the smallest acorn squash you can find. This recipe can be easily doubled or tripled.

1 ACORN SQUASH, HALVED
  AND SEEDED
2 TABLESPOONS UNSALTED
  BUTTER
2 TEASPOONS FIRMLY
  PACKED BROWN SUGAR
2 TABLESPOONS CURRANTS

Preheat the oven to 350 degrees. Prick the inside of the squash halves with a fork. Bake the squash in a baking dish for 45 minutes to an hour or until soft. Add 1 tablespoon butter, 1 teaspoon brown sugar, and 1 tablespoon currants to each squash half and mix well. Cook an additional 5 minutes.

Microwave-Poached Vanilla Pears

Makes 4 pear halves; Serves 2

2 PEARS, PREFERABLY
  BOSC
2 TEASPOONS FRESH
  LEMON JUICE
½ CUP SUGAR
½ CUP WATER
1 VANILLA BEAN, SPLIT
  LENGTHWISE

I always hated pears as a child. I am still not too fond of raw pears, but I love the texture and buttery flavor of poached pears. I used to poach pears in a saucepan, but I learned this easy microwave technique from <u>Dessert in Half the Time</u> by Linda West Eckhardt and Diana Collingwood Butts. It is so simple that sometimes I buy a bag of pears and poach them all at once. They can then be refrigerated, covered, and eaten as snacks throughout the next week. Bosc and Bartlett pears are the best varieties for poaching. Vanilla beans are expensive, but they can be reused many times. I keep a vanilla bean on hand just for this recipe. This recipe is best made at least 30 minutes in advance to give the pears time to cool. A nice holiday variation is to substitute cranberry juice for the water (omit the vanilla); the pears turn a pretty pale pink color.

Halve, peel, and core the pears. Sprinkle the freshly cut pears with the lemon juice to prevent browning. Place in a microwave-safe dish and sprinkle with the sugar. Add the water and vanilla bean. Cover and cook on High for 6 to 8 minutes or until the pears are fork tender. (Check the pears after 6 minutes; the fresher the pears, the longer they'll take to cook.) Spoon the syrup over the pears, cover, and let stand for 30 minutes or refrigerate overnight.

Easy Strawberry Sauce

Makes 1 cup

This easy sauce is pretty swirled on a dessert plate topped with poached pears. It's also a nice way to jazz up canned peaches.

1 CUP FROZEN STRAWBER-
RIES, THAWED, AT ROOM
TEMPERATURE
2 TABLESPOONS SUGAR OR
TO TASTE

Puree the strawberries and add the sugar. Chill until serving time.

Sparkling Grape Goblets

Serves 2

Serve this elegant nonalcoholic cocktail in the prettiest stemmed glasses you have.

½ CUP CHILLED GINGER
ALE
½ CUP CHILLED WHITE
GRAPE JUICE

Chill 2 wineglasses. At serving time, mix ¼ cup of the ginger ale and ¼ cup of the white grape juice in each of the prepared glasses.

HOLIDAY COOKING SHORTCUTS

1. The first rule of stress-free parties is that you don't have to make everything from scratch. Use staples such as high-quality ice creams, preshredded cheeses, frozen puff pastry and piecrusts, frozen bread doughs. I like to use those premixed salad greens; be sure to check the expiration date on them, though.

2. Fill up your freezer with homemade cookies or bread and appetizers for those last-minute guests. I like to keep some sugar cookie dough wrapped in plastic in the freezer for any last-minute party invitations or drop-in guests.

3. Go to your supermarket's salad bar and stock up on precut vegetables for your relish trays. Investigate the party trays and cheese trays and other take-out foods from your grocer's deli. Breakfasts and brunches are particularly easy to prepare for at your local grocery store; purchase pastries, doughnuts, and bagels from the bakery and add spreads, juices, granola, fruit, and yogurt for a wonderful menu.

4. If you just can't handle the thought of cooking for a crowd, consider a potluck or appetizer party so you won't have to spend the day cooking.

5. You can easily rent dinnerware, glassware, tablecloths, tables, chairs, napkins, punch bowls, ice buckets, coffee urns, and even chandeliers from your local rental agency. If you're not sure where to find such services, call a local caterer or meeting hall for advice.

6. Consider using a caterer for at least part of the party. Perhaps the caterer could provide only appetizers or a fancy dessert? Or if you like a particular dish from a local restaurant, consider purchasing some to go, to serve at your party. Another good idea is to consider hiring a high school student to help out by serving foods or cleaning up afterward.

7. Keep your pantry stocked throughout the holiday season to avoid unpleasant surprises. You are better off buying too many raisins than finding out at the last minute that you're all out. Try to keep some easy munchies on hand, such as pretzels, trail mix, dried fruits, and candy.

8. Ask for help from your family and friends. Perhaps your spouse or kids can tidy up the place while you're cooking? If you have any friends with a particular culinary talent, use it. If you ask someone to bring a dessert that is their specialty, they'll be flattered.

9. Since many people are worried about preparing desserts, consider something store-bought. A pound cake can be slightly reheated before serving so guests will think it is straight out of the oven. Serve with a fruit sauce and it is elegant and easy. Another dessert from the supermarket is ice-cream sundaes with all the trimmings, such as cherries, nuts, bananas, and hot fudge sauce.

Lively

TREE-TRIMMING
APPETIZER
Party

Hot Artichoke Heart Spread

Zesty Cheese Ball

Salted Rosemary-Garlic Braid

Quick Nacho Platter

Oven-Fried Zucchini Spears

Zesty Chipotle Mini-Muffins

Eggplant-Mushroom Bites

Frosted Chocolate Chip Bars

Hot Spiced Pineapple Tea

If I had to choose my favorite type of party to give, it would be an appetizer party. There is less pressure on the host or hostess, and most appetizers are easy to make and can be made wholly or partially in advance. This menu provides enough food to feed at least eight hungry tree-trimmers. Trimming the tree can be a big project, especially if you're like me and decorate more than one Christmas tree.

This past year I did the tree in the living room with only cat ornaments and I put a tree in the kitchen with food and cooking-related ornaments. If I had more space, I'd probably have a tree in every room in the house.

This appetizer menu is easy to do and will give you extra time to thread a string of cranberries or hang up some homemade gingerbread persons before the tree trimming begins. You'll need some good holiday music to get the ball rolling and get everyone into the holiday spirit.

Hot Artichoke Heart Spread

Makes about 1 cup; Serves 8

1 (4½-OUNCE) CAN MARI-
NATED ARTICHOKE HEARTS

¼ CUP GRATED ROMANO
CHEESE

¼ CUP PLAIN LOW-FAT
YOGURT

½ TEASPOON HOT-PEPPER
SAUCE

2 WHOLE-WHEAT PITA
BREADS, CUT INTO 4
PIECES

I like any recipe with artichoke hearts. They have a meaty, filling quality to them that is especially nice for vegetarians. I remember the first time I ate this spread; I was out to dinner with my father and it was served with pita bread wedges as an hors d'oeuvre. You can add some diced roasted sweet red peppers to this dish and serve it on French bread.

Preheat the oven to 375 degrees. Drain and chop the artichoke hearts. Add the Romano cheese, yogurt, and hot-pepper sauce. Put 2 tablespoons of spread on each pita bread wedge. Place on a baking sheet and bake for 15 minutes or until the cheese starts to melt. Serve hot.

Zesty Cheese Ball

Serves 8

Cheese balls are always popular at parties. I serve them accompanied by fruit and crackers. This is a pretty basic recipe, but you can vary it many ways by adding crushed pineapple or fresh herbs or chile peppers according to your taste. The exterior of the ball can be pressed with crushed cornflakes or minced nuts or colorful spices such as paprika.

1 (3-OUNCE) PACKAGE CREAM CHEESE, SOFTENED
¼ CUP MAYONNAISE
1 CUP GRATED GRUYÈRE CHEESE
1 CUP GRATED SHARP CHEDDAR CHEESE
¼ CUP DICED RED ONION
1 TEASPOON HOT-PEPPER SAUCE OR TO TASTE

Whisk together the cream cheese and mayonnaise. Add the Gruyère and Cheddar cheese and mix well. Add the remaining ingredients and shape into a ball. Wrap in plastic wrap and chill overnight.

Salted Rosemary-Garlic Braid

Makes 1 large braid

1 TABLESPOON ACTIVE DRY
  YEAST
¼ CUP WARM WATER,
  ABOUT 110 DEGREES
1 TABLESPOON HONEY
⅛ TEASPOON PLUS 1
  TABLESPOON SALT,
  DIVIDED
5 CLOVES GARLIC, MINCED
2 TABLESPOONS MINCED
  FRESH ROSEMARY
1 TABLESPOON OLIVE OIL
1¾ CUPS LUKEWARM
  WATER
3½ TO 4½ CUPS
  UNBLEACHED FLOUR

This is one of my favorite breads. Using a minimal amount of salt in the dough and sprinkling salt on the crust is a wonderful surprise. Please experiment with different types of salt until you find one you like; you'll be surprised at the differences. I use a sea salt bought in bulk at my health food co-op; coarse kosher salt is available at many supermarkets. Fresh rosemary is necessary to give this bread its wonderful aroma.

In the bowl of an electric mixer, dissolve the yeast in the ¼ cup warm water for 10 minutes. Add the honey, ⅛ teaspoon salt, garlic, rosemary, oil, and 1¾ cups lukewarm water. Mix with the beater blade of the mixer. Add the flour, 1 cup at a time. When the dough becomes thick, switch to the dough hook. Continue adding flour until the dough leaves sides of bowl. Knead for 10 minutes or until the dough is smooth and satiny.

Place the dough in an oiled bowl. Rotate the dough so that the entire surface is coated with oil. Cover with plastic wrap and let rise for 1¼ hours or until doubled.

Punch down the dough and divide into 3 equal pieces. Roll each piece out to a 12-inch length. Starting in the center, braid the loaf, tucking the pieces in at each end. Place on an ungreased baking sheet and cover with plastic wrap. Let rise for 45 minutes or until almost doubled. Preheat the oven to 400 degrees.

Sprinkle 1 tablespoon of the salt evenly over the braid. Bake for 30 to 40 minutes or until golden brown. Let cool on a rack.

Quick Nacho Platter

Serves 12

On busy weeknights, I often make up a big plate of nachos for dinner. It is a quick, simple meal and it is a nice accompaniment to a good old Christmas movie like <u>It's a Wonderful Life</u> or <u>Christmas in Connecticut.</u> I often mix blue and yellow corn tortilla chips for a prettier appetizer. Look for thick chips; they hold up better under the weight of the added goodies. If you make the recipe for Pickled Jalapeño Rings on page 198, you can use those for a topping.

1 (10-OUNCE) BAG ROUND CORN TORTILLA CHIPS
1 CUP REFRIED BEANS
1 CUP PREPARED SALSA
1 JALAPEÑO, SEEDED AND FINELY CHOPPED
1 MEDIUM TOMATO, DICED
6 SCALLIONS, THINLY SLICED
1 CUP GRATED COLBY CHEESE

On a pizza pan or cookie sheet, spread the tortilla chips in one layer. Add the beans and salsa in spoonfuls on top of the chips. Sprinkle with the jalapeño, tomato, scallions, and cheese. Broil 4 to 6 inches from the heat source until the cheese is melted, about 5 minutes.

Oven-Fried Zucchini Spears

Makes 36 spears; Serves 6

3 MEDIUM ZUCCHINI

2 EGGS

¼ CUP MILK

3 CLOVES GARLIC, CRUSHED

½ CUP UNBLEACHED FLOUR

½ CUP CORNMEAL

1 TEASPOON CHILI POWDER

½ TEASPOON ONION POWDER

½ CUP GRATED PARMESAN CHEESE

This is a great appetizer to serve with ranch or Thousand Island dressing, whether fresh or bottled. Bread the zucchini in advance, then cover and chill for several hours. Bake the wedges so they're ready when your party guests are assembled around the table. When making this (or any breaded vegetables) be sure to use the "one hand" method. Use one hand to dip the zucchini into the wet ingredients and the other hand to dredge it in the flour.

Preheat the oven to 425 degrees. Cut each zucchini in half, then each half lengthwise into 6 pieces or spears. Beat the eggs with the milk and add the garlic. In a separate bowl, mix the flour, cornmeal, chili powder, onion powder, and Parmesan cheese. Dredge the spears in the flour mixture, then coat with the egg mixture, then coat with the flour mixture again.

Place the spears on a greased cookie sheet and bake for 25 to 30 minutes or until golden brown. Serve hot.

Zesty Chipotle Mini-Muffins

Makes 24 mini-muffins or 12 regular muffins

These light and tender muffins use chipotle chile peppers, which are smoked jalapeños. Chipotles in adobo sauce are available in small cans in Hispanic markets or in supermarkets in the southwestern United States. You can also mail-order them from the Chile Shop (see Mail-Order Sources, page 221). Dried chipotle chile peppers can be rehydrated in water and substituted for the chipotles in adobo sauce.

¼ TEASPOON BAKING SODA

¾ TEASPOON BAKING POWDER

¾ TEASPOON SALT

1 CUP CORNMEAL

2 EGGS

¾ CUP PLAIN LOW-FAT YOGURT

4 TEASPOONS VEGETABLE OIL

3 CHIPOTLE CHILE PEPPERS IN ADOBO SAUCE, DRAINED AND MINCED

¼ CUP SHREDDED CHEDDAR CHEESE

Preheat the oven to 425 degrees. Spray two 12-cup mini-muffin tins or 1 standard 12-cup muffin tin lightly with nonstick cooking spray. Mix the baking soda, baking powder, salt, and cornmeal together in a small bowl. In a separate bowl, beat the eggs with the yogurt and oil. Stir in the chipotles and cheese. Gently stir the egg mixture into the cornmeal mixture until just mixed. Fill the muffin cups three-quarters full with batter. Bake for 10 to 15 minutes for regular-size muffins, 7 to 10 minutes for mini-muffins.

Eggplant-Mushroom Bites

Makes about 18 appetizers

2 JAPANESE EGGPLANTS, PEELED AND CHOPPED INTO ½-INCH PIECES (ABOUT ½ POUND EGG-PLANT)

4 OUNCES MUSHROOMS, CHOPPED INTO ½-INCH PIECES

1 TEASPOON SALT

3 TABLESPOONS OLIVE OIL

1 CUP FRESH WHOLE-WHEAT BREAD CRUMBS

⅓ CUP GRATED PARMESAN CHEESE

2 TABLESPOONS CHOPPED FRESH BASIL OR 2 TEA-SPOONS DRIED

These little morsels are addictive and will not last long. If you can't find Japanese eggplants, regular eggplant will work just fine. These appetizers can be mixed and shaped several hours ahead of time and broiled when your guests arrive.

Put the chopped eggplant and mushrooms in a colander and sprinkle with the salt. Let sit for 30 minutes. Pat the vegetables dry with a paper towel. In a nonstick skillet, sauté the vegetables over medium-high heat in the olive oil for 8 to 10 minutes or until they are soft.

Remove from the skillet with a slotted spoon and mix with the bread crumbs, Parmesan cheese, and basil. Use your hands to mix everything and form into 1-inch balls. Broil 4 inches from the heat source until golden brown. Turn the balls over and brown on the other side. Serve immediately.

Frosted Chocolate Chip Bars

Makes 25 bars

Tossing chocolate chips over the hot bars makes a quick and easy frosting. (You can also use this trick for frosting brownies.) These cookies travel well and keep nicely. In fact, the flavor improves over time, so you can make these a day ahead of the party with no worries.

Preheat the oven to 350 degrees. Lightly grease a 9-inch square pan.

With an electric mixer, cream the butter and brown sugar. Add the egg and mix well. Mix in the milk and vanilla. In a separate bowl, whisk together the flour, baking powder, and baking soda. Mix the dry ingredients with the wet and stir in 1 cup of the chocolate chips and all the walnuts. Spread the mixture in the prepared pan.

Bake for 30 to 40 minutes or until a toothpick inserted comes out clean. Immediately sprinkle with the remaining 1 cup chocolate chips and wait 5 minutes. Use a spatula to spread the chocolate chips over the top. Let cool completely and cut into bars.

½ CUP UNSALTED BUTTER, SOFTENED
¾ CUP FIRMLY PACKED BROWN SUGAR
1 EGG
2 TABLESPOONS MILK
1½ TEASPOONS VANILLA EXTRACT
1½ CUPS ALL-PURPOSE FLOUR
½ TEASPOON BAKING POWDER
⅛ TEASPOON BAKING SODA
2 CUPS SEMISWEET CHOCOLATE CHIPS, DIVIDED
½ CUP CHOPPED WALNUTS

Hot Spiced Pineapple Tea

Serves 8

I serve this hot fruity tea in red and green mugs. If desired, you can garnish each cup with an additional cinnamon stick.

Heat the water and pineapple juice in a saucepan until it boils. Add the cloves, cinnamon, lemons, and honey and lower the heat. Simmer 10 minutes over medium heat. Remove the cloves and cinnamon and serve hot.

4 CUPS WATER
4 CUPS PINEAPPLE JUICE
2 TEASPOONS WHOLE CLOVES
4 STICKS CINNAMON
4 LEMONS, HALVED AND SLICED
¼ CUP HONEY

100 Percent Natural

1. Fill a basket with pinecones, beeswax candles, oranges, and red bows for a pretty decoration. Or, even easier, fill a basket with pinecones and lemons.

2. A gourmet store near here sells the most beautiful holiday garlands made of bay leaves, dried cranberries, cinnamon sticks, dried apples, and kumquats. These simple garlands can dress up a window or door or can be hung on the Christmas tree. What is even better is that these garlands provide wonderful aromas for your home in addition to looking good.

3. I always try to remember to do something special for the wildlife at Christmas. Some easy treats for the birds, squirrels, and deer are pinecones spread with peanut butter, stale donuts hung on string, orange halves, and strings of cranberries and popcorn. If it is a particularly cold or snowy day, I sometimes make a batch of corn bread and crumble it up under a pine tree. The birds really seem to love this the best.

4. Although it seems impossible to keep them looking good after the holidays, every year I buy poinsettias to decorate my home. Nothing is more cheerful than a group of three or four poinsettias next to the fireplace or on the kitchen counter.

5. I like to make small bowls of homemade potpourri for my kitchen. I usually just throw together some cinnamon sticks, whole cloves and allspice, citrus peel, and pinecones. Put one bowl in the center of your stove top, since the heat will make the aroma stronger.

6. I always try to jazz up my punch bowl at large parties by surrounding the bowl with whole fruit, pinecones, and evergreen swags.

7. Pick out a Yule log this Christmas. Look for a really large piece of firewood, one big enough to burn the whole night on Christmas Eve. Wrap it with fresh herb sprigs and cotton twine and set it in a place of honor near the fireplace until Christmas Eve.

8. Baby's breath looks lovely bunched together in a basket and illuminated by dozens of tiny white lights.

5

Elegant
CHAMPAGNE
Dinner Party

Hot Deviled Nuts

Italian Fennel Salad

Balsamic Marinated Oranges

Overnight Mushroom Pâté

Herb and Cheese Braid

Red Onion Relish

Vegetable Stew with Puff Pastry Crust

Chocolate Yule Log

Champagne

I think serving champagne makes guests feel pampered. This is a nice late-night dinner party menu for adults only. Use only candles and Christmas lights to illuminate the house and ask your guests to dress up for the occasion. Put on some classical music. After dinner you and your guests can go on a moonlit tour of the neighborhood to view all the Christmas decorations, and return for dessert.

When choosing champagne, figure on about 1 bottle for two people. I serve champagne in flutes and I always give one of my guests the dubious honor of opening the bottle.

Hot Deviled Nuts

Makes about 5 cups

½ CUP UNSALTED BUTTER

2 TABLESPOONS VEGETAR-
IAN WORCESTERSHIRE
SAUCE

1 TEASPOON HABANERO
OR OTHER HOT-PEPPER
SAUCE

1 TEASPOON SALT

¼ TEASPOON ONION POW-
DER

¼ TEASPOON GARLIC POW-
DER

2 CUPS PECAN HALVES

3 CUPS ROASTED PEANUTS

This recipe makes a lot of nuts, but I like to have extra on hand for unexpected guests. You can fill up pretty champagne flutes with this mixture for a nice party favor. I buy vegetarian Worcestershire sauce (made without anchovies) at my local health food store. If you can't find it, substitute soy sauce in this recipe. This mixture keeps for about a month in a covered container at room temperature.

Preheat the oven to 375 degrees. Spray a cookie sheet with nonstick cooking spray. In a small saucepan, melt the butter and stir in the Worcestershire sauce, hot-pepper sauce, salt, onion powder, and garlic powder. Mix with the pecans and peanuts and spread in a single layer on the prepared cookie sheet.

Bake for 20 minutes or until the nuts are toasted and fragrant. Drain on paper towels.

Italian Fennel Salad

Serves 6

I prefer the taste of raw fennel to cooked because cooking can tone down its crisp anise flavor. This salad is best served immediately.

Slice the fennel bulb thinly and place in a serving dish. Add about 2 tablespoons finely minced fennel greens. Add the remaining ingredients and mix. Serve immediately.

1 LARGE FENNEL BULB (ABOUT 1 POUND), GREEN LEAVES RESERVED
1 TEASPOON SALT
3 TABLESPOONS EXTRA-VIRGIN OLIVE OIL
1 TABLESPOON RED WINE VINEGAR
1 SMALL RED ONION, THINLY SLICED
2 OUNCES Parmigiano-Reggiano, SLICED INTO ½-INCH PIECES

Balsamic Marinated Oranges

Serves 4 to 6

This simple dish can be made in advance. If you are looking for a way to use the orange peel discarded in this recipe, see the Candied Citrus Peel recipe on page 199.

Place the orange slices in a serving dish. Stir together the balsamic vinegar and brown sugar and pour over the oranges. Mix well and chill before serving.

4 NAVEL ORANGES, PEELED, HALVED, AND THINLY SLICED
3 TABLESPOONS BALSAMIC VINEGAR
1 TABLESPOON FIRMLY PACKED BROWN SUGAR

Overnight Mushroom Pâté

Makes about 1 cup

8 OUNCES MUSHROOMS,
  SLICED
1 MEDIUM ONION,
  CHOPPED
2 TABLESPOONS UNSALTED
  BUTTER
2 TABLESPOONS SOY
  SAUCE
1½ TEASPOONS GROUND
  CUMIN
SALT AND FRESHLY
  GROUND BLACK PEPPER
  TO TASTE
FRESH PARSLEY SPRIGS,
  FOR GARNISH

Serve this spread in a small ceramic bowl garnished with fresh parsley sprigs and surrounded by sliced homemade bread, toast points, or crackers.

Sauté the mushrooms and onion in the butter over low heat about 10 minutes or until the mushrooms release their juices. Puree the mixture in a food processor until finely chopped. Stir in the soy sauce and cumin and season with salt and pepper. Spread in a serving dish. Cover and refrigerate overnight. Garnish with the parsley immediately before serving.

Herb and Cheese Braid

Makes 1 large braid

This flavorful bread is always popular at parties and makes a nice addition to a gift basket. It needs only butter as an accompaniment for a wonderful snack.

1 TABLESPOON ACTIVE DRY YEAST

¼ CUP WARM WATER (ABOUT 110 DEGREES)

1 TABLESPOON SUGAR

3 CUPS UNBLEACHED FLOUR

½ CUP GRATED GRUYÈRE CHEESE, DIVIDED

2 TABLESPOONS GRATED PARMESAN CHEESE

1½ TEASPOONS SALT

¼ TEASPOON FRESHLY GROUND BLACK PEPPER

1½ TEASPOONS DRIED OREGANO

½ TEASPOON DRIED BASIL

2 TABLESPOONS OLIVE OIL

1 TABLESPOON HOT-PEPPER SAUCE, SUCH AS TABASCO

1 CUP LUKEWARM WATER

In a bowl of an electric mixer, dissolve the yeast in the warm water for 10 minutes. With the beater blade of the mixer, add the sugar, flour, cheeses (reserving 2 tablespoons of the Gruyère cheese), salt, black pepper, oregano, and basil. Switch to the dough hook attachment. Add the oil, hot-pepper sauce, and lukewarm water slowly. Knead until smooth and satiny, about 10 minutes.

Place the dough in an oiled bowl. Rotate the dough so that the entire surface is coated with oil. Cover with plastic wrap and let rise for 1½ hours or until doubled in bulk. Punch down the dough and let rest for 10 minutes.

Preheat the oven to 375 degrees. Divide the dough into 3 pieces and roll each piece into a 15-inch length. Braid, starting from the center. Tuck the ends under. Place on a baking sheet sprayed with nonstick cooking spray and cover with plastic wrap. Let rise for 45 minutes or until almost doubled in bulk.

Uncover and sprinkle with the reserved Gruyère. Bake for 25 to 30 minutes or until golden brown and the braid sounds hollow when tapped on the bottom.

Red Onion Relish

Makes 3 cups

10 JALAPEÑO OR SERRANO CHILE PEPPERS, SEEDED AND CHOPPED

1 MEDIUM RED ONION, THINLY SLICED

4 CLOVES GARLIC, THINLY SLICED

¼ CUP EXTRA-VIRGIN OLIVE OIL

¼ CUP APPLE CIDER VINEGAR

1 TEASPOON SALT

2 TEASPOONS DRIED OREGANO

This is one of my favorite condiments. Make it a day ahead to let the heat mellow slightly. It is also delicious served with enchiladas or egg dishes. Mexican oregano is stronger than regular (Greek) oregano and is great if you can find it.

Mix all the ingredients together in a serving dish. Cover and chill overnight. Stir before serving.

Vegetable Stew with Puff Pastry Crust

Serves 8

This savory stew is one of my favorite winter recipes. In this incarnation, I've topped it with an elegant puff pastry crust, but it is also delicious served plain or with a simple biscuit topping.

Sauté the onion and garlic in the oil for 5 minutes over medium heat or until tender. Stir in the flour until completely mixed. Add the vinegar, brown sugar, and mustard. Stir in the broth, cinnamon, carrots, and potatoes. Bring to a boil, reduce the heat, and simmer until thickened and the vegetables are tender, about 45 minutes. Add the peas and corn and cook an additional 10 minutes. (The recipe can be made ahead to this point.)

Preheat the oven to 350 degrees. Spray a 2-quart casserole dish with nonstick cooking spray. Spoon in the vegetable stew and let cool slightly. On a floured board, roll out the puff pastry sheet to a 12-inch square. Cut the pastry to fit the top of the casserole dish and place on top of the stew. Bake the casserole, uncovered, until the pastry is golden brown on top, about 20 to 30 minutes.

1 MEDIUM ONION, COARSELY CHOPPED

3 CLOVES GARLIC, MINCED

3 TABLESPOONS VEGETABLE OIL

3 TABLESPOONS UNBLEACHED FLOUR

2 TABLESPOONS APPLE CIDER VINEGAR

1 TABLESPOON FIRMLY PACKED BROWN SUGAR

2 TABLESPOONS PREPARED BALLPARK-STYLE MUSTARD

3 CUPS VEGETABLE BROTH

½ TEASPOON GROUND CINNAMON

2 LARGE CARROTS, CHOPPED (ABOUT 1 CUP)

2 LARGE POTATOES, PEELED AND CHOPPED (ABOUT 2 CUPS)

1 CUP FRESH OR FROZEN PEAS

1 CUP FRESH OR FROZEN CORN KERNELS

1 SHEET FROZEN PUFF PASTRY, THAWED FOR 20 MINUTES AT ROOM TEMPERATURE

Chocolate Yule Log

Serves 10

Cake

6 EGGS, SEPARATED
½ CUP SUGAR
6 OUNCES SEMISWEET
  BAKING CHOCOLATE
3 TABLESPOONS STRONG
  BREWED COFFEE
1 TEASPOON VANILLA
  EXTRACT

Filling

½ CUP WHIPPING CREAM
2 TABLESPOONS SUGAR
1 TEASPOON VANILLA
  EXTRACT

Topping

2 TABLESPOONS CONFEC-
  TIONERS' SUGAR
2 TABLESPOONS UNSWEET-
  ENED COCOA POWDER

I couldn't do a Christmas cookbook without including a recipe for a <u>bûche de noël,</u> or Yule log. I think they look so pretty on any holiday table. This one is a simple version, without the usual buttercream frosting and filling. The best thing about having a simpler recipe is that you can spend more time on the decorations! Meringue mushrooms or marzipan holly leaves and berries are all terrific ideas to spruce up this log. Merckens dark chocolate can be ordered from the Sweet Celebrations catalog or the King Arthur Flour Baker's Catalogue. It is a very rich-tasting chocolate with an incredibly smooth texture.

Preheat the oven to 350 degrees. Butter a 13-by-18-inch sheet cake pan and line with either aluminum foil or baking parchment. Butter the foil or parchment paper well.

To make the cake: Beat the egg yolks with the ½ cup sugar. Melt the baking chocolate in the coffee in a double boiler over lightly simmering water. Immediately remove from the heat and fold in the beaten egg yolks and add the vanilla extract.

With an electric mixer, beat the egg whites until stiff peaks form. Fold in the chocolate mixture and spread the batter evenly in the prepared baking pan. Bake for 15 minutes or until a toothpick inserted comes out clean. Take a tea towel and immerse it in water and squeeze dry. Grabbing the aluminum foil, pull the cake out of the pan and put it on top of the tea towel, foil and all. Gently roll up the cake and foil, starting with a short side, removing the tea towel as you go. Let cool 15 to 20 minutes.

To make the filling: Whip the cream until stiff and add the sugar and vanilla. Keep chilled until ready to use.

To make the topping: Sift together the confectioners' sugar and cocoa.

Carefully unroll the cake and spread with the whipped cream filling. Gently roll up again using the foil, removing the foil as you roll. Place the Yule log on a platter. Sift the topping over it. Use a fork to make swirls in the topping to look like the bark of a tree. Add marzipan leaves and berries if you desire. Chill before serving.

CREATIVE DECORATIONS

1. For a really dramatic table, try a dark green tablecloth with metallic glitter sprinkled lightly over the top. Add a few candles and let the glitter reflect the glow of the flames.

2. I like to decorate a little Christmas tree with food-related decorations. First I use a string of chile pepper lights, then I add wooden apples, whole heads of garlic tied with a red ribbon, a string of cranberries and popcorn, and tiny pomanders made with kumquats and cloves. (To make inserting cloves into citrus fruits easier, peel a thin strip around the fruit and then insert whole cloves.)

3. Ribbons and bows are one of the easiest decorations. String long ribbons from the center of your dining room table and let the ribbons drape down the table's sides for a dramatic look. Tie bows around silverware, around wineglasses, and on the backs of your chairs. One year I got really carried away and even tied tiny red bows in all my hanging houseplants. (It took forever to remove the bows after Christmas!)

4. This past year I put a sleigh bell decoration on my front door. You'd be amazed at how much better you feel each time you hear bells when you are entering or leaving your home. Don't stop there—tie bells on gifts, on glassware, even on your pets' collars, for a really entertaining Christmas.

5. If you can't find Christmas napkins you like, make your own! Fabric stores always have a nice selection of holiday fabrics and all you need to do is cut 18-inch squares of a pretty fabric and sew a ¼-inch hem for easy homemade napkins.

6. Buy some gold or silver spray paint and spray some pinecones and whole walnuts. Spray some bay leaves and sprinkle them around the table for a touch of shine.

7. I have a collection of really large pinecones that I painted. Use a large brush and just paint the tips white to resemble snow. These are pretty in a basket or just scattered around the kitchen table.

8. Decorate a cactus! Buy a small string of chile pepper lights and a few silk flowers to attach to the end of your cactus for a whimsical southwestern decoration.

9. Put Christmas ornaments in unexpected places. Hang them from a window shade pull, from a shower curtain, from a curtain rod, from doorknobs, from the ceiling, or in a doorway.

10. Use a lot of Christmas lights in all colors and sizes. String them around mirrors, in your table centerpiece, in houseplants, or anywhere else you can imagine.

11. I saw a pretty decoration in a magazine that consisted of a tiny evergreen placed in a copper pot for a stand. It was decorated completely with pasta—pasta was strung together for a garland and various pasta shapes were glued together to make flowers.

6

A SOUTHWESTERN Christmas Fiesta

Zucchini-and-Hominy Soup

Whole-Wheat Flour Tortillas

Carrot Salsa

Green Chile Enchiladas

Olé Corn

Green Beans with Piñon Nuts

Apricot-Almond Empanaditas

Orange Sherbet

Mexican Coffee

Christmas in the Southwest is a wonderful time, with deep purple sunsets and snow in the mountains. _Farolitos_ (paper bags filled with candles) line the streets on Christmas Eve and _luminarias_ (bonfires) are lit to represent the shepherds' fires in Bethlehem. Strings of dried chile peppers hanging in front of adobe homes are frosted with snow. Decorating a town with _farolitos_ is no easy project; in my hometown dozens of volunteers spend from dusk to midnight Christmas Eve lighting the candles to illuminate the downtown area.

This menu is designed to serve eight people. It can be served in the traditional style following midnight mass or as a simple weekday meal in December. All the recipes in this menu can be made in advance except the enchiladas, which should be baked when your guests arrive.

Zucchini-and-Hominy Soup

Serves 8

1 MEDIUM ONION, DICED

3 CLOVES GARLIC, MINCED

2 TABLESPOONS VEG-
ETABLE OIL

4 MEDIUM ZUCCHINI,
SLICED

1 CUP CHOPPED CANNED
OR FROZEN MILD GREEN
CHILE PEPPERS

6 CUPS VEGETABLE BROTH

4 CUPS COOKED YELLOW
HOMINY OR 2 (16-
OUNCE) CANS

1 TEASPOON GROUND
CUMIN

This is a vegetarian version of _posole,_ a dish made by Pueblos and Hispanics for feast days and special celebrations. Serve it with buttered homemade flour tortillas (recipe follows). Every fall I buy 20-pound bags of fresh New Mexico green chile peppers and have them roasted when I purchase them (at a supermarket or local farm stand). Then I freeze them whole in plastic bags. They are very easy to peel later when I'm ready to use them. To roast chile peppers yourself, cook them whole on the grill or under the broiler, turning occasionally, until charred and blackened. Let cool and freeze. You can save the task of peeling, seeding, and chopping them for later. Once the chiles are thawed, the peel removes very quickly.

Sauté the onion and garlic in the oil for 3 to 5 minutes. Add the zucchini and green chiles and cook over medium heat, stirring occasionally, another 5 minutes. Add the remaining ingredients and simmer, covered, over low heat for 45 minutes.

Whole-Wheat Flour Tortillas

Makes 12 (10-inch) tortillas

If you've never tasted homemade tortillas, you're in for a real treat. I prefer the taste of whole-wheat flour tortillas to white and these are perfect to serve warm with butter as an accompaniment to the Zucchini-and-Hominy Soup.

In a medium bowl, combine the flours, baking powder, and salt. Cut in the shortening until thoroughly combined. Gradually add the water and toss together until the dough can be gathered into a ball. Knead the dough for several minutes. Divide the dough into 12 balls. Cover with a tea towel and let rest in a warm place for 15 minutes.

On a lightly floured surface, roll each ball into a 10-inch circle. Cook the tortillas one at a time in an ungreased medium-hot skillet until browned on one side. Turn and cook the second side about 1 minute or until the edges start to curl. Wrap the warm tortillas in foil until all 12 have been cooked.

2 CUPS UNBLEACHED FLOUR
2 CUPS WHOLE-WHEAT PASTRY FLOUR
1½ TEASPOONS BAKING POWDER
1½ TEASPOONS SALT
¼ CUP VEGETABLE SHORT-ENING
1½ CUPS VERY WARM WATER (ABOUT 125 DEGREES)

Carrot Salsa

Makes 3 cups

This colorful salsa spices up any meal. Serve it with bean dishes, egg dishes, or tortilla chips.

Mix all the ingredients together in a serving dish. Chill for 1 hour before serving.

1 LARGE CARROT, GRATED
½ MEDIUM RED ONION, DICED
¼ CUP CHOPPED CANNED OR FROZEN MILD GREEN CHILE PEPPERS
1 CLOVE GARLIC, MINCED
2 TOMATOES, CHOPPED
1 TEASPOON FRESH LIME JUICE
1 TEASPOON SALT

Green Chile Enchiladas

Makes 12 enchiladas

These vegan enchiladas are always popular at a party. The tortillas can be filled and the sauce prepared ahead of time. For the filling, I use preroasted and peeled Bueno green chile peppers, which can be found in the freezer sections of supermarkets in the Southwest. If fresh or frozen green chile peppers are not available, substitute canned green chile peppers.

Sauce

3 CLOVES GARLIC, CRUSHED

2 TABLESPOONS VEGETABLE OIL

1 TABLESPOON DRIED OREGANO, PREFERABLY MEXICAN

2 TABLESPOONS GROUND CAYENNE PEPPER

2 TABLESPOONS UNBLEACHED FLOUR

1 (6-OUNCE) CAN TOMATO PASTE

3 CUPS WATER

1 TEASPOON SALT

1 TABLESPOON APPLE CIDER VINEGAR

Filling

1 MEDIUM RED ONION, DICED

3 TO 5 CLOVES GARLIC, MINCED

2 TABLESPOONS VEGETABLE OIL

1 TEASPOON GROUND CUMIN

1 CUP CHOPPED CANNED OR FROZEN MILD GREEN CHILE PEPPERS

2½ CUPS COOKED PINTO BEANS

12 (10-INCH) FLOUR TORTILLAS

To make the sauce: Sauté the garlic in the oil for 3 to 5 minutes in a saucepan. Add the oregano and cayenne and cook another 3 minutes. Add the flour and stir until all the oil is absorbed. Add the tomato paste and water slowly, stirring constantly, and cook over low heat until thick. Add the salt and vinegar.

To make the filling: Sauté the onion and garlic in the oil for 5 minutes or until soft. Add the cumin, green chiles, and pinto beans and cook over medium heat, mashing with a potato masher, about 5 minutes or until the consistency of a thick paste.

Preheat the oven to 350 degrees. Spoon about ¼ cup filling onto each tortilla, roll up, and place in a greased baking pan. Pour 2 cups sauce over the enchiladas and bake for 15 to 20 minutes or until bubbling. Heat the remaining sauce and serve with the enchiladas.

Olé Corn

Serves 8

This colorful and easy-to-prepare dish is an unusual way to serve corn that your guests will love.

Cook the corn in the water until tender. Add the chile peppers and olives and mix well. Serve hot.

4 CUPS FROZEN CORN
  KERNELS
½ CUP WATER
½ CUP CHOPPED CANNED
  OR FROZEN MILD GREEN
  CHILE PEPPERS
¼ CUP CHOPPED GREEN
  OLIVES

Green Beans with Piñon Nuts

Serves 8

If you can't find piñon nuts, also called pine nut or pignoli, substitute walnuts in this savory dish. One mail-order source for piñon nuts is Casados Farms (see Mail-Order Sources, page 221).

Sauté the onion, garlic, and chiles in the oil until soft. Add the green beans and piñon nuts. Cover and cook until tender, about 5 minutes.

1 LARGE ONION, DICED
3 CLOVES GARLIC,
  CRUSHED
¼ CUP CHOPPED CANNED
  OR FROZEN MILD GREEN
  CHILE PEPPERS
2 TABLESPOONS VEG-
  ETABLE OIL
2 POUNDS GREEN BEANS,
  TRIMMED AND CUT INTO
  1-INCH PIECES
½ CUP PIÑON NUTS

Apricot-Almond Empanaditas

Makes 16 empanaditas

1 SHEET FROZEN PUFF PASTRY, THAWED FOR 20 MINUTES AT ROOM TEMPERATURE

ABOUT 1 CUP APRICOT PRESERVES

¼ CUP SLIVERED ALMONDS

⅛ TEASPOON GROUND CINNAMON

CONFECTIONERS' SUGAR FOR DUSTING EMPANADITAS

Using frozen puff pastry makes short work of empanaditas. These are best when served immediately but can be filled in advance and refrigerated until serving time. I have never managed to completely thaw frozen puff pastry at room temperature for 20 minutes like the package states; it is best to put the box in the refrigerator the night before to thaw.

Preheat the oven to 400 degrees. Spray a cookie sheet with nonstick cooking spray. On a floured board, roll out the puff pastry sheet to a 12-inch square. Cut into 16 (3-inch) squares. In a small bowl, mix the apricot preserves with the almonds and cinnamon.

Top each square with a heaping teaspoon of the apricot preserve mixture. Fold the squares in half to form triangles. Brush the edges of the triangles with water and press the edges together with the tines of a fork. Place the triangles on the prepared baking sheet.

Bake the empanaditas for 15 minutes or until puffed and golden brown. Transfer to a wire rack and dust with confectioners' sugar. Serve warm.

Orange Sherbet

Makes about 1 quart

This creamy sherbet has a fresh orange flavor and scent and is a refreshing dessert after eating hot, spicy foods. For an attractive presentation, serve the sherbet in a hollowed-out orange half or a balloon glass. When squeezing the oranges, try to include some pulp.

1½ CUPS FRESH ORANGE JUICE (ABOUT 5 ORANGES)
2 TABLESPOONS FRESH LEMON JUICE
2 TEASPOONS GRATED ORANGE ZEST
⅔ CUP SUGAR
1½ CUPS LOW-FAT MILK OR SOY MILK

Combine all the ingredients and chill. Freeze in an ice-cream maker according to manufacturer's instructions. After the sherbet is frozen, let the mixture "ripen" for at least an hour in the refrigerator before serving. This makes the sherbet softer and easier to eat.

Mexican Coffee

Serves 8

Add 1 cinnamon stick, broken into 3 pieces, to freshly ground coffee and brew 8 cups in your coffee maker. Serve with milk and sugar. Hot chocolate can also be prepared with ground cinnamon for a hot children's drink.

DRESSED-UP DRINKS

1. If you don't have a punch bowl, consider tying a wide red bow around a large earthenware bowl or crystal bowl instead.

2. Freeze peeled, sliced kiwifruit or halved berries and use them for fruity ice cubes.

3. Use a tube pan, Bundt pan, or any type of decorative mold to make ice rings for your punches. Fill with citrus slices, cranberries, and other sliced or quartered fruit. Fill the pan or mold with fruit juice and freeze. This ice ring will keep your punch chilled and flavor it also.

4. Make plenty of ice cubes in advance of your party and store them in plastic freezer bags.

5. Fruit punches (without any sparkling waters or wines) can be mixed ahead of time for convenience.

6. Always have some nonalcoholic drinks on hand. Fruit juices, flavored seltzer water, and sparkling cider are all good choices.

7. Make sure you have plenty of glasses before your party. Plan on more than one per person, since sometimes people will drink more than one beverage at a party. Also buy plenty of lemons and limes.

8. I always plan on serving coffee late in the evening at any party. It is a good idea to offer it to your guests, especially those who have a long drive home. Remember to make sure you have milk or cream and sugar also.

7

Family Reunion
SANDWICH
CELEBRATION

Carrot-Peanut Butter Celery Slices

Cottage Cheese Salad

Sprouthead Sandwich

Spicy Rainbow Slaw

Open-Faced Herbed Pepper Sandwiches

Easy Veggie Cheeseburgers

Zucchini-Raisin Cookies

Hot Maple Nog

I am a great fan of sandwiches and I feel that they are a wonderful vegetarian meal. You don't need meat to be able to make a great sandwich. This easy make-ahead menu is perfect for those hectic family reunions where everyone is busy catching up and bouncing babies and showing Grandma and Grandpa how much they've grown. These sandwich and salad recipes, all of which can be prepared in advance, will be appreciated by all the generations at your celebration. Drag out the old photos and keep a camera handy for this party.

Carrot-Peanut Butter Celery Slices

Makes 16 appetizers

8 RIBS CELERY
½ CUP CREAMY NATURAL
  PEANUT BUTTER
1 CUP GRATED CARROTS
2 TABLESPOONS HONEY

Adding carrots and honey to peanut butter makes this a special kid's treat. You can use this spread for sandwiches too; try tossing in a few raisins.

Cut the celery into 4-inch-long pieces. Cut the pieces in half lengthwise. Mix the peanut butter with the carrots and honey. Fill the celery sticks with the peanut butter mixture. Chill until serving time.

Cottage Cheese Salad

Serves 8

2 POUNDS SMALL-CURD
  COTTAGE CHEESE
5 SCALLIONS, CHOPPED
2 MEDIUM GREEN BELL
  PEPPERS, DICED
2 MEDIUM CARROTS, THIN-
  LY SLICED
¼ CUP MINCED FRESH
  PARSLEY

This simple salad can be served on a bed of greens or sprouts.

Mix all the ingredients together gently. Cover and refrigerate for several hours before serving.

Sprouthead Sandwich

Makes 4 sandwiches

This sandwich is the recipe of Chris Mitchell, a vegetarian friend of mine from Nevada. He says that the tahini helps seal the bread and the sandwich travels well if carefully wrapped. I love it and it is a perfect vegan lunch box filler.

Spread 1 tablespoon of the tahini on each slice of bread. Add 1 leaf of Romaine lettuce, several slices of tomato, avocado, and onion, and ¼ cup sprouts per sandwich. Cover with another slice of bread. Slice and eat.

½ CUP TAHINI

8 SLICES WHOLE-WHEAT OR 7-GRAIN BREAD

4 LEAVES ROMAINE LETTUCE

1 MEDIUM TOMATO, THINLY SLICED AND PATTED DRY

1 AVOCADO, PEELED, PITTED, AND THINLY SLICED

1 SMALL RED ONION, THINLY SLICED

2 CUPS ALFALFA SPROUTS

Spicy Rainbow Slaw

Serves 6

4 CUPS THINLY SLICED
GREEN CABBAGE

1 PINT CHERRY TOMATOES,
QUARTERED

1 MEDIUM GREEN BELL
PEPPER, THINLY SLICED

1 SMALL RED ONION,
THINLY SLICED

2 LARGE CARROTS, THINLY
JULIENNED

2 TABLESPOONS SALT

1 CUP APPLE CIDER VINE-
GAR

⅓ CUP HONEY

1 TEASPOON CELERY SEED

½ TEASPOON GROUND
TURMERIC

¼ TEASPOON GROUND ALL-
SPICE

¼ TEASPOON GROUND CIN-
NAMON

¼ TEASPOON GROUND GIN-
GER

¼ TEASPOON GROUND
CLOVES

¼ TEASPOON CAYENNE

Don't be intimidated by the number of ingredients in this spicy, fat-free salad. Sprinkling the vegetables with the salt wilts them slightly and makes this coleslaw ready to eat right away.

In a colander, mix the cabbage, tomatoes, bell pepper, onion, and carrots and sprinkle with the salt. Let sit for 1 hour. Rinse the vegetables and drain well.

Mix the vinegar, honey, and spices and toss with the vegetables. Cover and chill a few hours before serving.

A Victorian Christmas Tea
Page 25

Romantic Yuletide Candlelight Dinner
Page 39

Elegant Champagne Dinner Party
Page 65

A Southwestern Christmas Fiesta
Page 79

Family Reunion Sandwich Celebration
Page 91

Christmas Open House
Page 125

Southern Christmas Eve Buffet
Page 141

Traditional New England Holiday Dinner
Page 165

Open-Faced Herbed Pepper Sandwiches

Makes 8 open-faced sandwiches

This recipe uses <u>herbes de Provence,</u> a mixture of dried marjoram, thyme, savory, basil, rosemary, sage, fennel seed, and lavender. I used bottled roasted sweet red and yellow peppers for this recipe to save time.

4 SLICES SOURDOUGH
SANDWICH BREAD
2 TABLESPOONS OLIVE OIL
3 TABLESPOONS CREAM
CHEESE, SOFTENED
3 CLOVES GARLIC, MINCED
2 TABLESPOONS CHOPPED
WALNUTS
½ TEASPOON FRESHLY
GROUND BLACK PEPPER
⅓ CUP SLIVERED ROASTED
RED AND YELLOW BELL
PEPPERS
1½ TEASPOONS *HERBES DE
PROVENCE*

Preheat the oven to 400 degrees. Spray a cookie sheet with nonstick cooking spray. Cut the slices of bread in half diagonally. Brush the slices with the olive oil. Spread with the cream cheese and top with the remaining ingredients. Place on the prepared cookie sheet and bake for 10 to 12 minutes or until the bread is crisp and the cheese has melted.

Easy Veggie Cheeseburgers

Makes 10 (½-inch) burgers

1 MEDIUM LEEK, RINSED
WELL AND DICED

3 CLOVES GARLIC, MINCED

2 TABLESPOONS UNSALTED
BUTTER OR OLIVE OIL

1 (16-OUNCE) CAN GAR-
BANZO BEANS, RINSED
AND DRAINED

2 CUPS COOKED LONG-
GRAIN BROWN RICE

1 TEASPOON SALT

10 SLICES AMERICAN
CHEESE

10 HAMBURGER BUNS

This is my all-purpose burger mix. It can also be used to make vegetarian meatballs by shaping the mixture into 1-inch balls and baking at 400 degrees for 20 minutes or until golden and firm. I like to serve these burgers with a slice of cheese on hamburger buns. You can vary the flavoring by adding curry powder or chili powder to the mixture if you like your burgers spicy. Be sure to drain the beans well, as any moisture will make the burger mix harder to shape. Also, after cooking the rice, I place a tea towel over the saucepan and re-cover to absorb any additional moisture.

Sauté the leek and garlic in the butter for 3 to 5 minutes or until cooked. Mix with the beans, rice, and salt. With a potato masher or food processor, puree until coarsely chopped or until the mixture just forms a ball and holds its shape well. Shape into ten 2½-inch burgers. Spray a nonstick skillet with cooking spray. Cook the burgers over medium heat for several minutes on each side until golden brown. Top the burgers with the cheese and continue cooking until the cheese has melted. Serve on the hamburger buns.

Zucchini-Raisin Cookies

Makes about 36 cookies

No one will guess these moist cookies contain zucchini. These freeze and ship quite well.

Preheat the oven to 325 degrees. Spray 2 cookie sheets with non-stick cooking spray. Mix the flour, oats, baking soda, salt, and spices together. Cream the butter with the brown sugar and add the egg. Mix until well blended. Stir the flour mixture into the creamed mixture and add the zucchini and raisins. Drop the mixture by heaping teaspoonfuls onto the prepared cookie sheets. Bake for 15 to 18 minutes or until golden brown. Cool on a wire rack before serving.

1½ CUPS WHOLE-WHEAT FLOUR
½ CUP OLD-FASHIONED OATS
1 TEASPOON BAKING SODA
½ TEASPOON SALT
½ TEASPOON GROUND CINNAMON
½ TEASPOON GROUND NUTMEG
¼ TEASPOON GROUND ALLSPICE
½ CUP UNSALTED BUTTER, SOFTENED
1 CUP FIRMLY PACKED BROWN SUGAR
1 EGG, BEATEN
1 CUP GRATED ZUCCHINI (ABOUT 1 MEDIUM ZUCCHINI)
1½ CUPS RAISINS

Hot Maple Nog

Serves 6

This simple hot drink is a real kid pleaser. I like to serve it with a cinnamon stick in each mug, but you can also sprinkle red hot cinnamon candies on top of each serving.

Over medium-low heat, cook the milk and maple syrup until heated through. Stir in the ground cinnamon and allspice and serve hot. Garnish with the cinnamon sticks.

6 CUPS MILK
1 CUP PURE MAPLE SYRUP
2 TEASPOONS GROUND CINNAMON
2 TEASPOONS GROUND ALLSPICE
6 STICKS CINNAMON, FOR GARNISH

8

Last-Minute SING-ALONG Party

Easy Cream of Tomato Soup

Parmesan Muffins

Confetti Couscous

Cranberry Waldorf Salad

Spicy Potato Slices

Chocolate-Mint Snowballs

Cranberry Seltzer

Here is a menu you can put together at the last minute. Nothing requires any exotic ingredients; all the recipes use foods that would normally be found in your pantry. Use this menu for when neighbors stop by unexpectedly with a gift for you or when friends stop over before a Christmas concert. I like singing Christmas carols, although I'm pretty weak on the lyrics. If you'd like to host a Christmas sing-along, check out the local library for a songbook containing the words to all your favorite holiday songs.

Easy Cream of Tomato Soup

Serves 4

1 LARGE LEEK, RINSED
WELL AND MINCED
3 CLOVES GARLIC, MINCED
2 TABLESPOONS UNSALTED
BUTTER
2 (28-OUNCE) CANS
WHOLE PEELED TOMA-
TOES, UNDRAINED
1 BAY LEAF
2 (12-OUNCE) CANS EVAP-
ORATED SKIM MILK
SALT AND FRESHLY
GROUND BLACK PEPPER
TO TASTE
FRESH BASIL LEAVES, FOR
GARNISH

If you haven't substituted evaporated skim milk for heavy cream in a recipe yet, do try it in this one. It adds a creamy texture without the fat. You can always keep a supply on hand in your pantry.

Sauté the leek and garlic in the butter in a Dutch oven over medium heat for 5 minutes or until tender. Add the tomatoes and liquid and bay leaf and crush the tomatoes slightly with a spoon. Cover and cook over medium-high heat for 15 minutes. Remove the bay leaf and puree. Add the milk and return to low heat and gently warm. Season with salt and pepper. Garnish with basil leaves.

Parmesan Muffins

Makes 12 muffins

These light, savory muffins are great with soup or whenever you need a quick bread for dinner.

2 CUPS UNBLEACHED
  FLOUR
2 TABLESPOONS BAKING
  POWDER
1 TEASPOON SALT
1 TABLESPOON SUGAR
½ CUP GRATED PARMESAN
  CHEESE
1 TEASPOON DRIED BASIL
1¼ CUPS MILK
1 EGG
¼ CUP UNSALTED BUTTER,
  MELTED

Preheat the oven to 400 degrees. Spray a 12-cup muffin tin with nonstick cooking spray. Whisk together the flour, baking powder, salt, sugar, Parmesan cheese, and basil. In a separate bowl, mix the milk, egg, and melted butter. Gently stir the wet and dry ingredients together. Fill the muffin cups three-quarters full. Bake at 400 degrees for 20 minutes or until lightly browned. Cool on a wire rack 15 minutes before serving.

Confetti Couscous

Serves 4

1 MEDIUM RED BELL PEP-
  PER, CHOPPED
1 MEDIUM GREEN BELL
  PEPPER, CHOPPED
1 MEDIUM RED ONION,
  CHOPPED
1 MEDIUM ZUCCHINI,
  CHOPPED
2 TABLESPOONS OLIVE OIL
5 CLOVES GARLIC,
  COARSELY CHOPPED
3 CUPS VEGETABLE BROTH
1½ CUPS COUSCOUS
SALT AND FRESHLY
  GROUND BLACK PEPPER
  TO TASTE

Preheat the oven to 425 degrees. Spray a 9-by-13-inch baking dish with nonstick cooking spray. Mix the peppers, onion, zucchini, olive oil, and garlic and spoon into the baking dish. Bake for 20 minutes, stirring occasionally, or until the vegetables are tender.

Meanwhile, bring the vegetable broth to a boil. Add the couscous, bring back to a boil, cover, and remove from the heat. Let steam for 10 minutes. Mix the couscous with the roasted vegetables and stir well. Season with salt and pepper.

Cranberry Waldorf Salad

Serves 4 to 6

1 CUP CRANBERRIES,
CHOPPED

2 TABLESPOONS SUGAR

2 LARGE APPLES, PEELED,
CORED, AND FINELY
CHOPPED

1 TABLESPOON FRESH
LEMON JUICE

3 RIBS CELERY, THINLY
SLICED

½ CUP CHOPPED WALNUTS

¼ CUP MAYONNAISE

This recipe doubles easily and is served chilled. Sweet apples like Fuji, McIntosh, and Delicious work best.

Toss the cranberries with the sugar to mix. Sprinkle the chopped apples with the lemon juice to prevent browning. Mix the cranberries and apples with the remaining ingredients. Cover and chill several hours before serving.

Spicy Potato Slices

Serves 6 to 8

These tongue-tingling slices are a delicious alternative to high-fat chips.

Preheat the oven to 425 degrees. Spray a 9-by-13-inch baking dish with nonstick cooking spray. Mix the melted butter with the chili powder, hot-pepper sauce, salt, and Parmesan cheese. Toss this mixture with the potato slices and spoon into the prepared dish. Bake, turning once, for 20 minutes or until golden brown.

2 TABLESPOONS UNSALTED BUTTER, MELTED

½ TEASPOON CHILI POWDER

1 TABLESPOON HOT-PEPPER SAUCE

1 TEASPOON SALT

¼ CUP GRATED PARMESAN CHEESE

4 BAKING POTATOES, PEELED AND THINLY SLICED

Chocolate-Mint Snowballs

Makes about 2 dozen snowballs

2 (6-OUNCE) PACKAGES
SEMISWEET CHOCOLATE
CHIPS
1 (15-OUNCE) CAN
SWEETENED CONDENSED
MILK
1 TEASPOON PEPPERMINT
EXTRACT
1 CUP CHOPPED WALNUTS
2 CUPS FLAKED COCONUT

I remember making these cookies with my mother when I was about ten years old. They are a lot of fun for kids to make because you have to get your hands messy and covered with chocolate to form the balls. I like to add mint extract to this, but they are also nice flavored with orange or almond. The best coating is coconut because they really do look like little snowballs, but you can also roll the cookies in ground nuts or confectioners' sugar. These are attractive served in tiny fluted paper candy cups.

Over low heat in a heavy saucepan, melt the chocolate chips and the sweetened condensed milk together. Stir in the peppermint extract and walnuts and let the mixture cool in the refrigerator for about 30 minutes or until easy to shape. Form the mixture into 1-inch balls and roll in the coconut. Chill before serving.

Cranberry Seltzer

Makes 6 tall drinks

1 QUART CRANBERRY
JUICE, CHILLED
1 QUART SELTZER,
CHILLED

My husband and I drink this all the time. I find the flavors go well with a variety of foods.

In tall glasses filled one-third full with ice, mix equal parts cranberry juice and seltzer.

CRANBERRIES, CRANBERRIES, CRANBERRIES

1. Try adding chopped cranberries to your usual pancake or waffle batter.

2. Ever had hot cranberry juice? It is a nice treat served with a cinnamon stick as a stirrer. Also, you can mix equal parts cranberry juice and apple cider for another simple hot drink.

3. Cranberries aren't just for eating. Fill shallow bowls with cranberries and insert a white votive candle for a colorful decoration.

4. Make ice cubes from cranberry juice for a versatile drink addition. Use them in sparkling water, ginger ale, orange juice, or lemon-lime soda. They are also pretty in a punch bowl.

5. Mix equal parts cranberry relish and orange marmalade for a tangy ice-cream topping or bread spread.

6. Use whole berry cranberry sauce in peanut butter sandwiches, as a cheesecake topping, as a filling for winter squash, or as an English muffin spread.

7. Dip fresh whole cranberries in light corn syrup and roll in granulated sugar. Let dry in a single layer on waxed paper and then use for a pretty plate garnish.

8. Fill baked puff pastry shells with whole berry cranberry sauce and top with whipped cream for a simple, easy dessert.

9. Toss cantaloupe cubes and green grapes with cranberry juice for an easy, colorful fruit salad.

Holiday
NEIGHBORHOOD
Potluck

Tortellini Parmesan Salad

Nutty Basmati Rice Salad

Down-Home Roasted Vegetables

Squash Cloverleaf Rolls

Two-Potato Jarlsberg Gratin

Chocolate Chip Cookies with Everything

White Chocolate-Cranberry Muffins

Crock-Mulled Spiced Cider

These simple dishes are ideal to bring to a potluck-style dinner and will be welcomed by all the guests. While they were created mainly for bringing to the potlucks we are all invited to, these dishes can be made all together for one stress-free, make-ahead menu.

I really like potlucks for a lot of reasons. First of all, they are less expensive for the host or hostess. Potlucks require less work, and I think people like to contribute and sample recipes from all the guests.

One really good tip for having a potluck is to do a little advance planning. Assign the guests different courses to bring, or you could end up with a table full of desserts or a dinner of only salads. For guests that don't cook, ask them to bring beverages, breads, or store-bought desserts.

Tortellini-Parmesan Salad

Serves 6

1 (16-OUNCE) PACKAGE
FRESH REFRIGERATED
CHEESE TORTELLINI

2 TABLESPOONS EXTRA-
VIRGIN OLIVE OIL

1 TABLESPOON RED WINE
VINEGAR

2 CLOVES GARLIC, MINCED

¼ CUP CHOPPED FRESH
BASIL OR 1 TABLESPOON
DRIED

¼ CUP GRATED PARMESAN
CHEESE

1 MEDIUM RED BELL PEP-
PER, DICED

FRESHLY GROUND BLACK
PEPPER TO TASTE

Pasta salads are always popular at potlucks. This salad of tortellini, red bell pepper, and green herbs is pretty and simple to make.

Cook the tortellini in boiling salted water according to package directions. Toss with the remaining ingredients. Cover and chill several hours or overnight.

Nutty Basmati Rice Salad

Serves 6

I just adore this salad and can often be found gobbling it down before it has even cooled.

In a serving dish, mix together the rice, scallions, carrots, sprouts, and raisins. In a small bowl, whisk together the peanut butter, olive oil, garlic, lemon juice, and hot-pepper sauce until smooth. Gently fold the dressing into the rice mixture. Cover and refrigerate overnight. Serve chilled or at room temperature.

2 CUPS COOKED LONG-
GRAIN OR BASMATI
BROWN RICE

3 SCALLIONS, DICED

2 MEDIUM CARROTS,
GRATED

½ CUP MUNG BEAN
SPROUTS, COARSELY
CHOPPED

½ CUP RAISINS

2 TABLESPOONS CREAMY
OR CHUNKY NATURAL
PEANUT BUTTER

1 TABLESPOON OLIVE OIL

1 CLOVE GARLIC, CRUSHED

1 TABLESPOON FRESH
LEMON JUICE

¼ TEASPOON HOT-PEPPER
SAUCE OR TO TASTE

Down-Home Roasted Vegetables

Serves 6

2 TABLESPOONS OLIVE OIL
2 MEDIUM RED POTATOES,
 PEELED AND CUT INTO
 ½-INCH PIECES
2 LARGE ONIONS, EACH
 CUT INTO 8 WEDGES
4 MEDIUM CARROTS, CUT
 INTO ½-INCH SLICES
6 CLOVES GARLIC

I really love the sweet, smoky flavor of roasted vegetables. This homey dish is both easy and filling. You can make this in advance, then take it to the potluck and heat it for 15 minutes at 350 degrees or serve it at room temperature.

Preheat the oven to 425 degrees. Spray a 9-by-13-inch baking dish with nonstick cooking spray. Mix all the ingredients together and spoon into the prepared dish. Bake for 50 minutes or until the vegetables are tender, stirring twice during cooking.

Squash Cloverleaf Rolls

Makes 18 rolls

I like to serve these savory golden rolls with Cranberry Butter (page 162).

1 POUND ACORN SQUASH, HALVED AND SEEDED

1 TABLESPOON ACTIVE DRY YEAST

¼ CUP WARM WATER (ABOUT 110 DEGREES)

1 CUP LUKEWARM WATER

2 TABLESPOONS VEGETABLE OIL

1 TABLESPOON PURE MAPLE SYRUP

1 TEASPOON SALT

¼ TEASPOON GROUND GINGER

2 CUPS WHOLE-WHEAT FLOUR

ABOUT 2½ CUPS BREAD FLOUR

Put the squash in a microwave-safe container, cover, and cook on High for 7 minutes or until tender when pierced with a fork. Remove from the shell, mash, and let cool. You should have about 1 cup pulp. In the bowl of an electric mixer, dissolve the yeast in the warm water for 10 minutes. Add the lukewarm water, oil, maple syrup, salt, ginger, and mashed, cooled squash. Add the whole-wheat flour. Slowly add the bread flour until a soft dough forms.

Knead until smooth and satiny, about 10 minutes, adding the bread flour as needed to prevent sticking. Oil a bowl and rotate the dough in the bowl to cover with oil. Cover with plastic wrap. Let rise in a warm place until almost doubled, about 1½ hours.

Gently punch down the dough and divide it into 54 pieces. Spray a 6-cup and a 12-cup muffin tin with nonstick cooking spray. Roll the dough into balls and place 3 balls in each muffin cup. Cover with plastic wrap and let rise for 30 minutes or until doubled. Preheat the oven to 375 degrees. Remove the plastic wrap and bake the rolls for 15 to 20 minutes or until golden brown.

Two-Potato Jarlsberg Gratin

Serves 4

2 LARGE YUKON GOLD POTATOES, PEELED AND THINLY SLICED

2 MEDIUM SWEET POTATOES, PEELED AND THINLY SLICED

4 CUPS VEGETABLE BROTH

1 TABLESPOON UNSALTED BUTTER

1 CLOVE GARLIC, CRUSHED

¾ CUP HEAVY CREAM

½ CUP GRATED JARLSBERG CHEESE

1 TEASPOON PAPRIKA, FOR GARNISH

This creative dish is always a favorite at parties; the combination of Yukon Gold potatoes, sweet potatoes, and nutty Jarlsberg is irresistible. To take this dish to a potluck, assemble and bake the casserole ahead, then reheat at 350 degrees for 15 to 20 minutes.

Preheat the oven to 375 degrees. Bring the potatoes and vegetable broth to a boil in a heavy saucepan. Lower the heat to medium and simmer for 10 minutes. Stir occasionally to prevent sticking. Drain. Rub a 1½-quart casserole dish with the butter and the crushed garlic. Stir the potatoes with the cream and Jarlsberg cheese and spoon into the prepared casserole. Sprinkle the top with the paprika. Bake for 1 hour or until the top is golden brown.

Chocolate Chip Cookies with Everything

Makes about 4 dozen cookies

These big cookies truly have everything. They freeze well and are a perfect gift. I have a beautiful Italian platter that I love to pile high with these cookies for parties. The secret to big chewy cookies is to form the dough into a ball and make sure the dough is chilled. If you have only two cookie sheets, make sure they cool down before baking another batch. Use a mild-flavored granola without any unusual additions if you can find it. I usually use a honey-nut variety.

½ CUP UNSALTED BUTTER, SOFTENED
¾ CUP FIRMLY PACKED BROWN SUGAR
1 EGG
1½ TABLESPOONS VANILLA EXTRACT
1 CUP UNBLEACHED FLOUR
¼ TEASPOON BAKING SODA
½ TEASPOON SALT
¼ TEASPOON BAKING POWDER
½ CUP FLAKED COCONUT
½ CUP GRANOLA
¾ CUP CHOPPED PECANS
¾ CUP CHOPPED CURRANTS
1¾ CUPS SEMISWEET CHOCOLATE CHIPS

Preheat the oven to 350 degrees. Spray cookie sheets with nonstick cooking spray. With an electric mixer, cream the butter and brown sugar. Add the egg and vanilla and beat well. In a separate bowl, whisk together the flour, baking soda, salt, and baking powder. Add to the wet ingredients along with the coconut, granola, pecans, currants, and chocolate chips. Stir until combined. Cover and chill the dough for 30 minutes in the refrigerator.

Drop by tablespoonfuls onto the prepared cookie sheets about 1½ inches apart. Bake for 10 to 15 minutes or until lightly browned. Immediately remove from the cookie sheets and cool on a wire rack.

FESTIVE CENTERPIECES

1. If you have a favorite crystal bowl, fill it with red and green satin Christmas balls. Another simple centerpiece is to group a collection of nutcrackers, teddy bears, or favorite ornaments together for a personalized table.

2. Gingerbread houses are one of my favorite centerpieces. If you like to make your own (or if you buy one already made), place it in the middle of the table. You can purchase small electric lights at hobby stores to illuminate the house from within or you can simply surround it with votive candles.

3. Gather together colorful autumn leaves, twigs, branches, and berries and spread them out over the table. Top with attractive winter squash, dried corn, and gourds.

4. Put some bare twigs in a vase and insert gumdrops or cranberries on the ends of the branches for an unusual tree centerpiece.

5. Remember to cut the lowest branches from your Christmas tree before you put it in water. Save these pine boughs and set them on the table in a random manner. Top with elegant Christmas ornaments and ribbons for a traditional holiday centerpiece.

6. Use a colorful rug as a table runner for a country look. Top with a selection of fruits, vegetables, and flowers.

7. A nice natural centerpiece can be made by lining a wooden bowl with colorful leafy greens. Fill with a selection of winter fruit. To make sure the fruit looks its very best, polish it with a soft cloth and a drop of vegetable oil.

8. If you are handy with wrapping paper, wrap up some empty boxes with all the trimmings and pile them in the center of your table. Or find a small Norfolk pine and decorate it just like a Christmas tree.

2 CUPS UNBLEACHED
FLOUR
½ CUP FIRMLY PACKED
DARK BROWN SUGAR
½ TEASPOON SALT
1 TABLESPOON BAKING
POWDER
1 CUP MILK
¼ CUP UNSALTED BUTTER,
MELTED AND ALLOWED TO
COOL SLIGHTLY
2 EGGS
1 CUP WHITE CHOCOLATE
CHIPS
1 CUP COARSELY CHOPPED
CRANBERRIES

White Chocolate–Cranberry Muffins

Makes 12 muffins

This recipe was created when I was reading a recipe for cookies with cranberries and white chocolate chips. I thought the idea might work even better in a muffin; I was right. These muffins are unlike most other muffins in that their flavor seems to improve the day after baking.

Spray a 12-cup muffin tin with nonstick cooking spray. Preheat the oven to 400 degrees. Whisk together the flour, brown sugar, salt, and baking powder. In a separate bowl, beat the milk, butter, and eggs together. Add the wet ingredients to the dry mixture, along with the white chocolate chips and cranberries, and fold together. Fill the muffin cups three-quarters full with batter. Bake for 18 to 20 minutes or until the muffins are golden brown. Cool on a wire rack before serving.

Crock-Mulled Spiced Cider

Serves 10

My best friend Mariellen makes hot spiced cider in her Crock-Pot for her annual Christmas Eve party. It keeps all night on a low setting, and she puts a bottle of Southern Comfort or other whiskey or rum next to the Crock-Pot for those who wish to add it. This cider is a portable and always popular recipe for potlucks.

7 CUPS APPLE CIDER OR APPLE JUICE
4 CINNAMON STICKS
1 TEASPOON WHOLE ALL-SPICE
1 TEASPOON WHOLE CLOVES
¼ CUP SUGAR

Mix all ingredients and stir well. Put mixture in a covered Crock-Pot on a low setting.

10

Christmas
OPEN HOUSE
for Fifty

Herb-Stuffed Snow Peas

Baked Broccoli Morsels

Sage Breadsticks

Skewered Vegetables and Cheese

Crock-Pot Chipotle and Black Bean Dip

Cheese Tortellini with Chunky Tomato Dip

Easy Layered Southwestern Dip

Artichoke Squares

Stuffed Dates

Smoky Chile-Cheese Balls

Blonde Brownies

Mini-Croquembouche

Easy Chocolate Chip Meringues

An open house is probably the easiest way to entertain. Having one big party fulfills all your holiday obligations, and an open house is normally a casual affair where people can drop by whenever they please. I've done only foods that can be eaten by hand for this menu, which makes the party even simpler. You won't even need to provide knives and forks!

When I host an open house, I grab my address book and the phone book and send invitations to everyone I know. I start planning the party several weeks ahead by browsing through my cookbooks and recipe files. I prepare as much food as possible a day or two ahead and I invite a close friend over as a helper the day of the party.

For beverages for a large party like this, I prefer to buy soda and flavored bottled waters. This saves you from having to provide glasses and you can fill a variety of large waterproof containers with ice for a simple serving idea. I also try to place bags or containers to collect recyclables in various spots around the house.

Herb-Stuffed Snow Peas

Makes about 40 appetizers

½ POUND FRESH OR
FROZEN SNOW PEAS,
BLANCHED
1 (8-OUNCE) PACKAGE
CREAM CHEESE, SOFT-
ENED
1 TABLESPOON FRESH
LEMON JUICE
1 CLOVE GARLIC, CRUSHED
1 TABLESPOON MINCED
FRESH MARJORAM
1 TABLESPOON MINCED
FRESH LEMON THYME
1 TABLESPOON CHOPPED
FRESH CHIVES (PREFER-
ABLY GARLIC CHIVES)
1 SCALLION, MINCED

This appetizer takes a bit of time but always disappears quickly at any party. If you can't find fresh marjoram, substitute fresh dill weed.

Using a paring knife, slit the snow peas on one side. Mix the remaining ingredients together and fill a pastry bag or a plastic bag with one corner clipped. Fill the peas. These can be covered, refrigerated, and stored for 2 to 3 days.

Baked Broccoli Morsels

Makes about 30 morsels

3 CUPS BLANCHED BROC-
COLI FLORETS, FINELY
CHOPPED
1 CUP GRATED MONTEREY
JACK CHEESE
1 CUP GRATED CHEDDAR
CHEESE
3 EGGS
5 SLICES WHOLE-WHEAT
BREAD, CRUMBLED
1 CLOVE GARLIC, CRUSHED
1 TEASPOON LEMON PEP-
PER

This is a fun way to serve broccoli. I think they taste good hot, at room temperature, or cold, but I wouldn't bake them too far in advance. You can, however, mix the ingredients and form the mixture into balls before the party.

Preheat the oven to 375 degrees. Spray a baking sheet with nonstick cooking spray. Mix all the ingredients together and shape into 1-inch balls. Place on the prepared baking sheet and bake for 15 to 20 minutes or until lightly browned.

Sage Breadsticks

Makes 40 breadsticks

These herbed breadsticks are thin and crispy. The best breadsticks are the ones that are stretched, not rolled. Serve these stacked high in a rustic basket lined with a red or green napkin.

1 TABLESPOON ACTIVE DRY YEAST
1 TEASPOON SUGAR
1 CUP WARM WATER (ABOUT 110 DEGREES)
1 TEASPOON SALT
2 TABLESPOONS OLIVE OIL
2 TABLESPOONS MINCED FRESH SAGE OR 2 TEA-SPOONS CRUMBLED DRIED
¼ CUP GRATED PECORINO ROMANO CHEESE
ABOUT 2½ CUPS UNBLEACHED FLOUR

Dissolve the yeast and sugar in the warm water for 10 minutes. Stir in the salt, olive oil, sage, and cheese. Add the flour slowly. Turn out the dough onto a well-floured board and knead 20 minutes or until smooth and satiny.

Oil a bowl and place the dough in it, turning the dough to cover with oil. Cover and let rise in a warm place for 30 minutes or until doubled in bulk. Punch down.

Preheat the oven to 400 degrees. On a floured board, roll the dough out to a 12-inch square. Sprinkle the dough lightly with additional flour. Divide the dough into 4 equal pieces. Cut each piece into 10 strips. Stretch each strip out to 12 or 15 inches long. Place ½ inch apart on a greased cookie sheet. Bake for 15 minutes or until golden brown and crispy. Serve hot or at room temperature.

Skewered Vegetables and Cheese

Makes about 30 appetizers

Use three different colored peppers for a particularly attractive presentation.

1 POUND COCKTAIL OR
PEARL ONIONS, PEELED
3 MEDIUM BELL PEPPERS,
CHOPPED INTO 1-INCH
PIECES
2 TABLESPOONS BALSAMIC
VINEGAR
2 TABLESPOONS OLIVE OIL
1 POUND PROVOLONE
CHEESE, CUT INTO 1-INCH
CUBES

Preheat the oven to 400 degrees. Spray a baking sheet with nonstick cooking spray. Mix the onions and peppers with the balsamic vinegar and olive oil. Spread in a single layer on the prepared baking sheet and bake for 20 minutes or until the vegetables are tender, stirring occasionally. Skewer the peppers and onions on bamboo skewers with the cheese and serve.

Crock-Pot Chipotle and Black Bean Dip

Makes about 7 cups

I use my miniature Crock-Pot for this, but an old fondue pot would work well, too. This dip can be mixed in advance. Serve it with plenty of corn or tortilla chips.

3 (16-OUNCE) CANS
BLACK BEANS, DRAINED
1 (16-OUNCE) CAN WHOLE
PEELED TOMATOES
3 CUPS DICED AMERICAN
CHEESE
3 CHIPOTLE CHILE PEP-
PERS IN ADOBO SAUCE,
DICED

Mash the beans slightly with a potato masher and cut up the tomatoes with scissors. Add the tomatoes, their juice, the cheese, and the chipotles to the beans. To heat, put in a Crock-Pot over low heat and stir until the cheese has melted.

HOW TO PLAN A PARTY

1. The most important part of giving a party is organizing. Make several lists—one with activities, one with your menu, one with groceries to be purchased, one with the guests you plan to invite.

2. Preplanning is important so you will have fun at your own party. Everything from choosing the music to arranging the centerpiece to picking out your clothes to setting the table can be done in advance.

3. Do try all new recipes before the party to avoid any unpleasant surprises. There is nothing worse than having a recipe disaster a half hour before the guests are due to arrive. Keep recipes simple; perhaps you can pick one complicated dish to serve such as a dessert, but if every dish is time-consuming and involved, you'll be a nervous wreck by the time your guests arrive.

4. Figure out ahead of time which serving dishes you are going to use for each food you are planning to serve. Plan table settings and other decorations several weeks before the party.

5. For a large buffet or open house, set up several stations in different parts of the house for serving food. This will keep people moving and make feeding everyone more efficient.

6. Consider how your guests will eat. Don't serve foods that are difficult to eat if your family and friends will have to do it standing up or perched on the end of a chair.

7. I always give myself at least a half hour before every party to relax. Either I invite a good friend over to wait with me for the arrival of the rest of the guests or I just try to sit down with a glass of wine and listen to some music to get in the mood before the party starts.

8. Keep a journal of all your parties so you can remember successes, failures, guests who didn't get along, menus, and to help you come up with your own time-saving tips. Also, keep a file folder of favorite holiday recipes and photos of table settings that appeal to you to help you in planning your next party.

Cheese Tortellini with Chunky Tomato Dip

Serves 12 as an appetizer

1 (16-OUNCE) PACKAGE
FRESH REFRIGERATED
CHEESE TORTELLINI

3 TABLESPOONS EXTRA-
VIRGIN OLIVE OIL,
DIVIDED

3 CLOVES GARLIC, MINCED

1 TEASPOON SALT

1 TEASPOON DRIED
OREGANO

1 (28-OUNCE) CAN WHOLE
PEELED TOMATOES

1 (9-OUNCE) PACKAGE
FROZEN ARTICHOKE
HEARTS, THAWED AND
COARSELY CHOPPED

8 *PEPERONCINI* (PICKLED
ITALIAN PEPPERS),
CHOPPED

The sauce for these little morsels can be made ahead and reheated at serving time. When ready to serve, spear two tortellini with a toothpick and arrange on a platter surrounding the warm dip. You can also mix the tortellini with the sauce for a fun light pasta meal.

Cook the tortellini in boiling salted water according to package directions. Immediately rinse in cold water and drain well. Toss with 1 tablespoon of the olive oil and cover and refrigerate. Skewer 2 tortellini per toothpick at serving time.

With the remaining 2 tablespoons oil, sauté the garlic for 3 minutes over medium heat. Add the salt and oregano. Coarsely chop the canned tomatoes and add the artichoke hearts and *peperoncini*. Stir the tomato mixture in with the sautéed garlic and cook, stirring occasionally, for 5 minutes or until the sauce begins to simmer. Puree the tomato sauce with a hand blender until it is well chopped. Serve warm with the tortellini.

Easy Layered Southwestern Dip

Makes about 5 cups

This familiar dip is easy to prepare and always welcome at a party. Serve it with yellow and blue tortilla chips.

Mash the avocados and stir in the lemon juice. Layer the avocados on a large serving platter with the salsa and cheese. With a rubber spatula, carefully spread the sour cream over the top. Decorate with the olives.

2 AVOCADOS, PEELED AND
  PITTED
1 TABLESPOON FRESH
  LEMON JUICE
1 (12-OUNCE JAR) PRE-
  PARED SALSA
1 CUP GRATED MONTEREY
  JACK CHEESE
1 CUP GRATED COLBY
  CHEESE
1 PINT SOUR CREAM
½ CUP SLICED GREEN
  OLIVES
½ CUP SLICED BLACK
  OLIVES

Artichoke Squares

Makes about 60 appetizers

These savory appetizer bars can be made a day in advance.

Spray an 8-inch square baking pan with nonstick cooking spray. Preheat the oven to 350 degrees. Drain the artichokes, reserving 2 tablespoons marinade. Sauté the onion and garlic in the marinade for 5 minutes. Let cool.

Mix the sautéed onion and garlic with the remaining ingredients. Pour into the prepared pan and bake for 30 minutes or until lightly browned. Let cool for 10 minutes and cut into 1-inch squares. Serve at room temperature.

2 (6-OUNCE) JARS MARI-
  NATED ARTICHOKE HEARTS
1 MEDIUM ONION, DICED
2 CLOVES GARLIC,
  CRUSHED
4 EGGS
1 SLICE WHOLE-WHEAT
  BREAD, CRUMBLED
½ TEASPOON DRIED
  OREGANO
2 TEASPOONS HOT-PEPPER
  SAUCE
2 CUPS GRATED CHEDDAR
  CHEESE

Stuffed Dates

Makes 24 dates

24 WHOLE DATES
2 TABLESPOONS ALMOND
  PASTE
¼ CUP CONFECTIONERS'
  SUGAR

Every Christmas my mother would stuff whole dates with pecans and roll them in confectioners' sugar. We never seemed to have these dates any other time of year, so they have a permanent Christmas association for me. I have taken her recipe and made it just a <u>little</u> richer. Almond paste should be available in the baking section of your grocery store. Look for relatively soft tubes and don't be daunted by the high price. It is so rich and flavorful that you'll only need a little for each recipe. I buy whole honey dates at my health food store for this recipe.

Make a lengthwise slit in each date and remove the pit. Fill each date with ¼ teaspoon almond paste and re-form the date around the filling. Roll the stuffed dates in the confectioners' sugar.

Smoky Chile-Cheese Balls

Makes about 32 (1-inch) balls

These miniature versions of the traditional cheese ball or log will disappear quickly.

Spray a cookie sheet with nonstick cooking spray. Mix the cream cheese with the smoked Cheddar, scallion, lemon juice, and chipotle chile pepper. Cover and chill for 15 minutes. Form the mixture into 1-inch balls, about 1 heaping tablespoon per ball. In a small shallow bowl, stir together the chili powder and oregano. Lightly roll each ball in the chili powder mixture and place on the prepared cookie sheet. Cover and chill before serving. Spear each ball with a toothpick before serving.

3 (8-OUNCE) PACKAGES CREAM CHEESE, SOFT-ENED

2 CUPS GRATED SMOKED CHEDDAR CHEESE

1 SCALLION, DICED

1 TABLESPOON FRESH LEMON JUICE

1 CHIPOTLE CHILE PEPPER IN ADOBO SAUCE, MINCED

2 TABLESPOONS CHILI POWDER

1 TEASPOON DRIED OREGANO

Blonde Brownies

Makes 24 bars

⅔ CUP UNSALTED BUTTER
(10⅔ TABLESPOONS),
SOFTENED

2 CUPS FIRMLY PACKED
BROWN SUGAR

2 EGGS

2 TEASPOONS VANILLA
EXTRACT

2 CUPS UNBLEACHED
FLOUR

½ TEASPOON SALT

2½ TEASPOONS BAKING
POWDER

½ CUP CHOPPED PECANS

1 (12-OUNCE) PACKAGE
BUTTERSCOTCH CHIPS,
DIVIDED

I've tried this recipe two different ways; with the butter-scotch chips mixed into the batter and with all the butter-scotch chips sprinkled on top. I could never decide which way I preferred, so I finally ended up doing it both ways. These bar cookies store and ship really well and are a welcome alternative to all the chocolate sweets I seem to make all the time around the holidays.

Preheat the oven to 350 degrees. Spray a 9-by-13-inch baking pan with nonstick cooking spray. In the bowl of an electric mixer, cream the butter and brown sugar. Add the eggs and vanilla and beat well. In a separate bowl, whisk together the flour, salt, and baking powder. Mix the dry ingredients with the wet and gently stir in the pecans and 1 cup of the butterscotch chips.

Pat the mixture into the prepared baking pan and sprinkle the remaining butterscotch chips on top. Bake for 30 to 40 minutes or until golden and the edges start pulling away from the sides of the pan. Cool on a wire rack and cut into squares.

Mini-Croquembouche

Serves 12

This is probably my favorite holiday dessert. Croquembouche means "crunch in the mouth" and is a French holiday dessert. Whenever I serve it, people get a kick out of pulling the cream puff balls from the "tree." This version is somewhat easier than the traditional one: the cream puff balls are filled with a spiced whipped cream instead of a custard, and a chocolate-butter glaze rather than a caramel one is used to hold the whole thing together. The smaller size of this croquembouche makes it a nice dessert for a family dinner. Unfortunately, croquembouches don't hold well and the chocolate glaze needs to be done at the last minute. The cream puff balls can be made in advance and kept refrigerated. Before serving, you'll need to whip the cream, fill the cream puffs, and make the chocolate glaze. Whenever I have to whip cream, I put both the bowl of my electric mixer and the whisk attachment in the freezer for at least 5 minutes. A pretty garnish for this dish is a few raspberries and some mint leaves placed around the tree.

Cream Puffs

1 CUP WATER
½ CUP UNSALTED BUTTER, CUT INTO 6 PIECES
1 CUP UNBLEACHED FLOUR
PINCH OF SALT
4 EGGS

Filling

1 CUP WHIPPING CREAM
¼ CUP CONFECTIONERS' SUGAR
½ TEASPOON FRESHLY GRATED NUTMEG
½ TEASPOON VANILLA EXTRACT

Chocolate Glaze

6 OUNCES SEMISWEET CHOCOLATE
¼ CUP UNSALTED BUTTER

To make the cream puffs: **P**reheat the oven to 400 degrees. **B**ring water and butter to a boil. **R**educe the heat to low and stir in the flour and salt. **A**dd the eggs, one at a time, stirring continuously until all the eggs are incorporated into the dough. Drop the dough by teaspoonfuls onto ungreased cookie sheets. With a wet finger, touch up any puff to make it round and smooth. Bake for 10 minutes or until puffed up and golden. Let cool slightly and with a sharp knife, cut a ½-inch slit in the bottom of each puff.

To make the filling: In a chilled bowl, whip the cream with the confectioners' sugar, nutmeg, and vanilla. One to 2 hours before serving, fill a pastry bag with the whipped cream filling and fit it with a round tip. Pipe the filling into each cream puff and refrigerate immediately.

To make the chocolate glaze: Melt the chocolate and butter in a double boiler over 1 inch of simmering water.

Take out a serving dish for the *croquembouche* and begin assembling a tree by putting about 6 filled cream puffs on the dish for the bottom layer. Use a drop of chocolate glaze to hold the cream puffs together. Continue adding cream puffs in a pyramid shape. When the *croquembouche* is assembled, dribble the remaining chocolate glaze over the whole tree. Garnish as desired.

Easy Chocolate Chip Meringues

Makes 2 dozen cookies

I often get a taste for meringues. They're relatively easy too, once you know how to make them properly; meringues need to be baked in a low oven and should not be browned. Although many meringue recipes have you use a pastry bag to pipe out pretty designs, I think they taste just as good dropped from a spoon. If you like, you can substitute dried cranberries or cherries for the chocolate chips for a totally nonfat cookie. I also sometimes use coarsely chopped unsweetened baking chocolate in place of the chocolate chips. The bitterness of the chocolate contrasts really well with the sweetness of the meringues, but they are more of a meringue for adults. This chocolate chip version will be loved by young and old alike. I use Von Snedaker's Magic Baking Sheets to line my cookie sheets. They are marvelous reusable Teflon-coated fiberglass sheets that can be cut to fit any size baking sheet. They are sold in the King Arthur Flour Baker's Catalogue (see Mail-Order Sources, page 221). You can also use baking parchment instead of the Magic Baking Sheets.

2 EGG WHITES, AT ROOM
TEMPERATURE
½ CUP SUGAR
½ TEASPOON VANILLA
EXTRACT
1 CUP SEMISWEET CHOCO-
LATE CHIPS

Preheat the oven to 250 degrees. Line cookie sheets with Magic Baking Sheets or parchment paper. Beat the egg whites until stiff peaks form. Continue beating and slowly add the sugar and vanilla until the mixture is stiff and glossy. Stir in the chocolate chips.

Drop the mixture by tablespoonfuls onto the prepared sheets. Bake for 45 minutes or until the meringues are crisp on the outside but still moist on the inside. If you want totally crisp meringues, turn off the oven after 45 minutes and leave in overnight.

11

Southern
Christmas Eve
BUFFET

Savory Peanut Soup

Mustard-Dill Coleslaw

Sweet Potato-Cranberry Salad

Buttermilk Corn Bread/
Corn Bread Dressing Ring

Savory Creamed Spinach

Hazelnut Green Beans

Easy Rice Pilaf

Green Chile-Cheese Bread

Stuffed Peaches

Lemon Cheesecake with Caramelized Lemon Zest

Iced Sun Tea with Mint

Christmas Eve is a good time for hosting a party because everyone is usually in a festive mood and ready to celebrate the season. A buffet is a nice way to serve dinner because guests don't all have to arrive at the same time and you don't have to serve everyone at one table. This is a menu with all the abundance of traditional southern buffets. All of the foods keep well at room temperature and this large feast can serve up to twelve people.

Savory Peanut Soup

Serves 12

10 SCALLIONS, SLICED,
PLUS ADDITIONAL FOR
GARNISH

4 RIBS CELERY, DICED

3 TABLESPOONS UNSALTED
BUTTER

3 TABLESPOONS
UNBLEACHED FLOUR

4 CUPS VEGETABLE BROTH

1 CUP EXTRA-CHUNKY NAT-
URAL PEANUT BUTTER

ROASTED PEANUTS, FOR
GARNISH

Serve this creamy soup over a hot plate or warmer.

In a heavy sauté pan, cook the scallions and celery in the butter for 5 minutes, stirring occasionally. Add the flour and stir until well blended. Slowly add the broth, stirring. Add the peanut butter and cook over low heat for 15 minutes. Garnish with roasted peanuts and sliced scallions.

Mustard-Dill Coleslaw

Serves 12

8 CUPS SHREDDED GREEN
CABBAGE

2 CUPS HALVED AND THIN-
LY SLICED RADISHES

⅔ CUP MAYONNAISE

2 TABLESPOONS PREPARED
MILD MUSTARD

2 TABLESPOONS WHITE
WINE VINEGAR

2 TEASPOONS SUGAR

1 TEASPOON CELERY SEED

2 TABLESPOONS MINCED
FRESH DILL OR 2 TEA-
SPOONS DRIED

SALT AND FRESHLY
GROUND BLACK PEPPER
TO TASTE

I use a honey mustard for this spicy coleslaw. It is best made a day in advance.

Mix the cabbage and radishes in a serving bowl. In a small bowl, mix the remaining ingredients. Add to the cabbage mixture, tossing gently to coat. Cover and chill overnight before serving.

Sweet Potato–Cranberry Salad

Serves 12

This lively salad is best served lukewarm.

Steam the sweet potatoes until tender, about 40 minutes. Add the onion and cranberries. In a small bowl, mix the mayonnaise with the lime juice and lime oil. Season with salt and pepper. Gently toss the dressing with sweet potato mixture.

2 POUNDS SWEET POTA-
TOES, PEELED AND
CHOPPED

1 LARGE RED ONION,
SLICED

1 CUP CHOPPED CRANBER-
RIES

¼ CUP MAYONNAISE

2 TABLESPOONS FRESH
LIME JUICE

2 DROPS LIME OIL OR 2
TEASPOONS GRATED LIME
ZEST

SALT AND FRESHLY
GROUND BLACK PEPPER
TO TASTE

Buttermilk Corn Bread

Makes 2 loaves

2 CUPS UNBLEACHED
  FLOUR
2 CUPS CORNMEAL
2 TABLESPOONS BAKING
  POWDER
2 TEASPOONS SALT
1 TEASPOON BAKING SODA
3 TABLESPOONS SUGAR
2 EGGS
3 CUPS BUTTERMILK
½ CUP UNSALTED BUTTER,
  MELTED AND COOLED
  SLIGHTLY

This recipe makes two loaves of corn bread, enough for the Corn Bread Dressing Ring on the facing page. This recipe freezes well. It can also be halved. I've tried many corn bread recipes and I think the butter in this makes all the difference in the world. I also use a small amount of sugar to improve the flavor. You can create many variations by adding one or more additional ingredients to the batter, like whole corn kernels, chopped jalapeño peppers, grated Cheddar cheese, and chili powder to taste.

Preheat the oven to 425 degrees. Spray two 8-inch-square baking pans or two 9-by-5-inch loaf pans with nonstick cooking spray. In a mixing bowl, combine the flour, cornmeal, baking powder, salt, baking soda, and sugar. Separately beat the eggs with the buttermilk and melted butter. Pour the wet ingredients into the dry ingredients and gently stir together. Don't overmix. Pour the batter into the prepared baking pans and bake for 20 to 25 minutes or until a toothpick inserted comes out clean. Let cool slightly before slicing and serving.

Corn Bread Dressing Ring

Serves 12

This main dish is baked in a Bundt pan for an attractive presentation. For a spicier flavor, add one or two chopped chipotle chile peppers in adobo sauce to the dressing.

Preheat the oven to 350 degrees. Spray a 12-cup Bundt pan with nonstick cooking spray. Mix all the ingredients together in a large bowl. Pat the ingredients into the prepared pan. Bake for 40 to 45 minutes or until lightly browned. Let cool for 15 minutes, then invert the pan onto a serving platter to remove the dressing ring.

6 CUPS CORN BREAD CRUMBLED INTO 1-INCH PIECES (1 RECIPE BUTTERMILK CORN BREAD, PAGE 146)

¼ CUP UNSALTED BUTTER, MELTED

4 RIBS CELERY DICED

8 SCALLIONS, DICED

1 MEDIUM GREEN BELL PEPPER, DICED

1½ CUPS CHOPPED PECANS

5 CLOVES GARLIC, MINCED

½ TEASPOON SALT

1 TEASPOON DRIED THYME

3 EGGS

1 CUP VEGETABLE BROTH OR WATER

Savory Creamed Spinach

Serves 12

2 MEDIUM LEEKS, RINSED
WELL AND THINLY SLICED
8 OUNCES MUSHROOMS,
FINELY CHOPPED
2 TABLESPOONS UNSALTED
BUTTER
4 CLOVES GARLIC, MINCED
2 (10-OUNCE) PACKAGES
FROZEN CHOPPED
SPINACH, THAWED
1 (8-OUNCE) PACKAGE
CREAM CHEESE, SOFT-
ENED
¼ CUP MILK
SALT TO TASTE

The mushrooms in this recipe add a bit more flavor than the usual creamed spinach recipes. This recipe can be made ahead and reheated for a few minutes in the microwave.

In a large skillet, sauté the leeks and mushrooms in the butter for 5 minutes, stirring occasionally. Add the garlic and sauté another 3 minutes. Add the spinach, cream cheese, and milk and stir over low heat until well mixed and warmed through. Season with salt.

Hazelnut Green Beans

Serves 12

2 POUNDS GREEN BEANS,
TRIMMED
¼ CUP UNSALTED BUTTER
10 SCALLIONS, SLICED
½ CUP CHOPPED HAZEL-
NUTS

Hazelnuts are my favorite nuts. Unfortunately, they are not always easy to locate where I live, so when I do find them, I buy them in bulk and store them well wrapped in the freezer.

Steam the green beans for 8 to 10 minutes or until tender-crisp. In a sauté pan, melt the butter. Add the scallions and cook 3 minutes over medium heat. Stir in the hazelnuts and green beans and cook until warmed through.

Easy Rice Pilaf

Serves 12

This is one of my favorite rice dishes. You can use converted brown rice for this dish to save some time. I also use it to stuff steamed bell peppers or zucchini.

Cook the rice in the water in a covered saucepan over medium heat until tender, about 40 minutes. Sauté the onion in the butter for 5 minutes. Add the garlic and continue to cook another 3 minutes, stirring occasionally. Add the corn and rice to the sautéed onion and garlic and cook for an additional 2 minutes. Season with salt and pepper.

2 CUPS LONG-GRAIN BROWN RICE
4 CUPS WATER
1 LARGE RED ONION, DICED
2 TABLESPOONS UNSALTED BUTTER
8 CLOVES GARLIC, MINCED
4 CUPS FRESH OR FROZEN CORN KERNELS
SALT AND FRESHLY GROUND BLACK PEPPER TO TASTE

Green Chile-Cheese Bread

Makes 2 loaves

1 TABLESPOON ACTIVE DRY YEAST

2 CUPS WARM WATER (ABOUT 110 DEGREES)

1 TABLESPOON SUGAR

1 CUP CHOPPED FROZEN OR CANNED MILD GREEN CHILE PEPPERS

2 TEASPOONS SALT

1 EGG, AT ROOM TEMPERATURE

3 CLOVES GARLIC, MINCED

1 CUP GRATED CHEDDAR CHEESE, DIVIDED

¼ CUP UNSALTED BUTTER, SOFTENED

ABOUT 5½ CUPS BREAD FLOUR

A local bakery makes a wonderful version of this bread studded with chiles and cheese. Because this is such a rich dough, I use bread flour to increase the dough's rise. My favorite way of shaping this bread is to divide the dough into three balls per loaf. All you do is put the three balls into your loaf pan and you get an attractively shaped loaf. This bread freezes well and the flavor improves overnight. I like to give these loaves away in my Christmas gift baskets, as they are a nice change from the usual sweet bread.

In a large bowl, dissolve the yeast in the warm water for 10 minutes. Stir in the sugar, chiles, salt, egg, garlic, ¾ cup of the Cheddar cheese, and the butter and mix well. Slowly add the flour until a soft dough forms. Knead for 20 minutes or until the dough is smooth and satiny.

Oil a bowl and place the dough in it, turning the dough to cover with oil. Cover and let rise in a warm place for 1½ hours or until the dough has doubled in bulk.

Preheat the oven to 400 degrees. Spray two 8½-by-4½-inch loaf pans with nonstick cooking spray. Punch down the dough and divide it into 6 pieces. Roll each piece into a ball and place 3 balls in each loaf pan. Cover with plastic wrap and let rise in a warm place for 45 minutes or until almost doubled in bulk.

Bake the loaves for 40 minutes or until golden and hollow when tapped on the bottom. Remove from the oven and place the loaves on a wire rack. Immediately sprinkle the loaves with the remaining ¼ cup cheese and let cook on rack before serving.

Stuffed Peaches

Serves 12

The new fruit-juice-sweetened spreads available make stuffing fruits quite easy. If you have trouble peeling the peaches, blanch them in boiling water for 1 minute using tongs and the peel will slip off easily.

6 LARGE PEACHES, HALVED, PEELED, AND PITTED
¼ CUP BLACKBERRY FRUIT SPREAD
¼ CUP SLIVERED ALMONDS

Fill each peach half with 1 teaspoon of blackberry fruit spread and sprinkle the almonds over all. This dish can be prepared several hours before serving and covered tightly.

Lemon Cheesecake with Caramelized Lemon Zest

Serves 12

Cheesecake

22 OUNCES CREAM
  CHEESE, SOFTENED
1¼ CUPS SUGAR
4 EGGS
½ CUP HEAVY CREAM
2 TEASPOONS VANILLA
  EXTRACT
⅛ TEASPOON LEMON OIL
  OR 2 TEASPOONS FINELY
  GRATED LEMON ZEST

Caramelized Lemon Zest

ZEST OF 2 LEMONS, CUT
  INTO SLIVERS
1 TEASPOON SUGAR
2 TABLESPOONS UNSALTED
  BUTTER

This creamy Manhattan-style crustless cheesecake is adapted from a recipe in Carole Walter's Great Cakes. The texture of this cheesecake is a little creamier than most, so I use a strand of dental floss to cut it into slices. The recipe for the caramelized lemon zest that tops this thick cheesecake is from The Von Welanetz Guide to Ethnic Ingredients by Diana and Paul Von Welanetz. I met Diana Von Welanetz through CompuServe's online service and she is a truly charming lady. Her lemon zest recipe elevates this cheesecake into a heavenly delight.

To make the cheesecake: Preheat the oven to 325 degrees. Butter a 9-inch springform pan. With an electric mixer, beat the cream cheese and sugar. Add the eggs, cream, vanilla, and lemon oil and continue beating just until smooth.

Pour the batter into the prepared pan. Surround the bottom of the pan with a large piece of aluminum foil to contain any leakage. Bake for 1 hour or until just firm. Turn off the oven and prop open the oven door with a wooden spoon. Keep the cheesecake in the oven for an hour. Remove from the oven and let cool at room temperature. Top with caramelized lemon zest. Chill before serving.

To make the caramelized lemon zest: Sauté the zest and sugar in the butter in saucepan over very low heat, stirring, until the sugar has melted. Drain on paper towels. Sprinkle the zest on top of cheesecake.

Iced Sun Tea with Mint

Serves 12

Iced tea is my favorite drink with southern menus. To make iced sun tea with mint, put 6 tea bags and 12 cups of water in a large glass container. Add about 1 cup of mint leaves and put the container in a sunny, warm spot for several hours. If you can't find fresh mint, you can cheat by using mint tea bags. I buy mint tea bags by either Bigelow or Lipton that are a combination of black tea and spearmint.

FUN WITH CANDY CANES

1. Use small candy canes as stirrers for hot chocolate, tea, or coffee.

2. Always keep a big bowl of candy canes to give out to people who come to the door—mail carriers, UPS delivery persons, neighbors.

3. Crush candy canes with a wooden mallet or hammer and add to basic sugar cookie dough or sprinkle on top of cookies before baking. Crushed candy canes are also a nice topper for vanilla ice cream.

4. Tuck a small candy cane with silverware and tie up with a red ribbon.

5. One idea I saw in an old magazine was to make a candy cane vase. Basically, you take an empty coffee can and glue candy canes, curved side up, around the entire can. Fill this with fresh red carnations for a spirited holiday decoration.

6. Tie candy canes together for an unusual garland.

12

Quick 'n' Easy CHRISTMAS Breakfast

Swiss Chard and Cheese Strata

Banana-Nut Muffins

Cranberry Butter

Broiled Skewered Mangoes

Baked Lemon Rice Pudding

Hot Spiced Tea

Christmas morning is probably the most hectic time for all of us, especially for those households with small children. If you can make a nice breakfast menu in advance, you may just be able to get a few extra winks of sleep. I love stratas and they are the perfect make-ahead breakfast or brunch recipe. The Hot Spiced Tea is also a nice treat for a snowy afternoon.

Swiss Chard and Cheese Strata

Serves 6 to 8

6 SLICES WHOLE-WHEAT BREAD

1 POUND SWISS CHARD STEMS AND LEAVES, CHOPPED

2 CUPS GRATED COLBY CHEESE

4 EGGS

2 CUPS MILK

2 TEASPOONS DIJON MUSTARD

This recipe can be changed by substituting any lightly steamed vegetable and any type of complementary cheese. It has to be prepared ahead of time and refrigerated, which makes it an ideal dish to bring to a potluck dinner or to make ahead for a lazy Sunday dinner.

Remove the crusts from the bread and fit the slices into a rectangular baking pan sprayed with nonstick cooking spray. Cover with the Swiss chard and press the grated cheese firmly down on top. In a separate bowl, beat together the eggs, milk, and mustard and pour over the casserole. Cover with plastic wrap and refrigerate 3 to 4 hours or overnight. Bake at 350 degrees for 45 to 50 minutes or until firm and puffy. Let stand 10 minutes before serving.

Banana-Nut Muffins

Makes 12 muffins

These muffins really taste a lot like the dried banana chips you can buy at your health food store. I haven't tried freezing them because they never last long enough for that!

1½ CUPS UNBLEACHED
FLOUR
½ CUP WHOLE-WHEAT PAS-
TRY FLOUR
1 TABLESPOON BAKING
POWDER
½ TEASPOON SALT
½ CUP CHOPPED WALNUTS
½ CUP UNSALTED BUTTER,
SOFTENED
1 CUP SUGAR
2 EGGS
3 RIPE BANANAS, MASHED
(ABOUT 1½ CUPS)

Preheat the oven to 400 degrees. Spray a 12-cup muffin tin with nonstick cooking spray. Mix the flours, baking powder, salt, and walnuts in a bowl. With an electric mixer, cream the butter and sugar until smooth. Add the eggs, one at a time, and beat well. Gently fold in the bananas. Mix the wet ingredients with the dry ingredients and stir just until mixed. Fill the muffin cups three-quarters full with batter. Bake for 20 minutes or until the tops are springy to the touch. Cook on a rack.

Cranberry Butter

Makes about 1 1/2 cups

1 CUP CRANBERRIES
1/2 CUP UNSALTED BUTTER,
  SOFTENED
1/2 CUP HONEY
1 TABLESPOON FRESH
  LEMON JUICE

Serve this tangy butter with quick breads, muffins, or pureed squash or root vegetables. You can also heat Cranberry Butter in the microwave until completely melted for a unique pancake or waffle syrup.

Puree the cranberries in a food processor or blender. Add the remaining ingredients and process until smooth.

Broiled Skewered Mangoes

Serves 4

1/4 CUP HONEY
JUICE OF 1 LIME
2 TABLESPOONS GRATED
  FRESH GINGER
2 MANGOES, PEELED AND
  CUBED

This is a wonderful treat for both children and adults. The fruit can also be broiled.

In a small bowl, stir together the honey, lime juice, and ginger. Add the mangoes and mix thoroughly. (You can also let the mangoes marinate in this mixture for several hours before broiling.)

Skewer the mangoes and broil 3 to 4 inches from the source of heat for 3 to 5 minutes, brushing with additional marinade at least once during broiling. If you have any marinade left over, serve it with the kabobs.

Baked Lemon Rice Pudding

Serves 6 to 8

Nothing is more comforting than a good rice pudding. You can prepare this the night before and bake it in the morning while you're sipping a hot cup of tea. If served warm, I like to top this with a dollop of yogurt or sour cream.

2 EGGS

2 CUPS MILK

⅓ CUP FIRMLY PACKED BROWN SUGAR

3 TABLESPOONS FRESH LEMON JUICE

2 DROPS LEMON OIL OR ½ TEASPOON GRATED LEMON ZEST

1 TEASPOON VANILLA EXTRACT

2 CUPS COOKED SHORT-GRAIN RICE

½ CUP GOLDEN RAISINS (OPTIONAL)

Preheat the oven to 350 degrees. Spray a 1½-quart baking dish with nonstick cooking spray. Beat the eggs, milk, brown sugar, lemon juice, lemon oil, and vanilla together. Stir in the rice and raisins if using. Bake for 50 to 60 minutes or until firmly set. Serve warm or chilled.

Hot Spiced Tea

Makes 8 cups

I serve tea more often than I serve coffee at parties. This recipe is best served as soon as possible after preparing.

8 CUPS WATER

6 BLACK TEA BAGS

1 STICK CINNAMON

4 WHOLE CLOVES

⅓ CUP SUGAR

2 ORANGES, SLICED

1 LEMON, SLICED

Bring the water to a boil. Add the remaining ingredients and simmer for 5 minutes. Remove the tea bags and spices and serve hot.

13

Traditional
NEW ENGLAND
HOLIDAY
Dinner

Creamy Squash, Apple, and Corn Bisque

Dill-Rye Bread

Garlic Mashed Potatoes

Tangy Zucchini Spears

Savory Bread Pudding

Rich Mushroom Gravy

Steamed Spinach

Cranberry-Orange Sauce

Carrot Cake with Maple Cream Cheese Frosting

Eggnog Ice Cream

Easy Orange Shakes

This dinner includes many of my favorite recipes. It also translates well for other holidays such as Thanksgiving or for family reunions, as the food is traditional enough to remind us all of our childhood holidays. This menu can serve a crowd, so you needn't worry if any unexpected guests show up at the last minute.

Creamy Squash, Apple, and Corn Bisque

Serves 6 to 8

1 POUND ACORN OR BUT-
TERNIT SQUASH, PEELED,
SEEDED, AND FINELY
CHOPPED (ABOUT 3
CUPS)

3 TART APPLES, PEELED,
CORED, AND FINELY
CHOPPED

3 TABLESPOONS UNSALTED
BUTTER

3 MEDIUM LEEKS, RINSED
WELL AND SLICED

1 CLOVE GARLIC, MINCED

4 CUPS VEGETABLE BROTH

1½ CUPS FROZEN CORN
KERNELS

6 TABLESPOONS HEAVY
CREAM

¼ TEASPOON FRESHLY
GRATED NUTMEG

4 SCALLIONS, FINELY
MINCED, FOR GARNISH

This thick, creamy soup can be cooked a day in advance and reheated gently before serving.

Over medium heat, sauté the squash and apples in the butter for 5 minutes, stirring occasionally. Add the leeks and garlic and sauté another 5 minutes. Add the broth and corn and simmer 10 minutes. Stir in the cream and nutmeg and heat just until warmed through. Sprinkle the bowls with the minced scallions. Serve hot.

Dill-Rye Bread

Makes 2 loaves

This is a sticky dough, but the results are worth it. Pure gluten flour can be purchased at health food stores; it is <u>not</u> the same as high-gluten flour or bread flour. An electric stand mixer such as the KitchenAid is essential for kneading this heavy dough.

1 TABLESPOON ACTIVE DRY
  YEAST
½ CUP WARM WATER
  (ABOUT 110 DEGREES)
3 TABLESPOONS HONEY
1½ CUPS LUKEWARM
  WATER
1 CUP PLAIN LOW-FAT
  YOGURT, AT ROOM TEM-
  PERATURE
2 TABLESPOONS OLIVE OIL
2 TEASPOONS SALT
1 TABLESPOON DILL SEED
¼ CUP CHOPPED FRESH
  DILL OR 1 TABLESPOON
  DRIED
3 CUPS RYE FLOUR
1 TABLESPOON PURE
  GLUTEN FLOUR
ABOUT 4½ CUPS
  UNBLEACHED FLOUR

In a bowl of an electric mixer, dissolve the yeast in the warm water and the honey for 10 minutes. Add the lukewarm water, yogurt, oil, salt, dill seed, and dill. Beat on low speed with the mixer beater until mixed. Add the rye flour and gluten and continue mixing.

Change to the dough hook and add the unbleached flour 1 cup at a time. Knead for 10 minutes on low speed. Put the dough in an oiled bowl, rotate to coat with oil, cover with plastic wrap, and let rise in a warm place about 1½ hours or until doubled. Punch down the dough and divide it in half.

Shape the dough into loaves and put each in a 9-by-5-inch loaf pan sprayed with nonstick cooking spray. Cover with plastic wrap. Let rise until almost doubled, about 45 minutes. Preheat the oven to 375 degrees. Bake the loaves for 45 minutes or until golden brown and a loaf is hollow when thumped.

Garlic Mashed Potatoes

Serves 10

Here is a recipe for mashed potatoes with a difference; you won't taste the horseradish, but it gives this dish zest and fullness.

6 LARGE RUSSET OR
YUKON GOLD POTATOES,
PEELED AND CUBED
6 CLOVES GARLIC
¼ CUP MILK, AT ROOM
TEMPERATURE
2 TABLESPOONS UNSALTED
BUTTER
½ TEASPOON SALT
¼ TEASPOON WHITE PEP-
PER
1 TEASPOON PREPARED
CREAMY HORSERADISH

Cook the potatoes and garlic cloves in boiling salted water for 25 to 30 minutes or until the potatoes are easily pierced with a fork. Drain well. In the bowl of an electric mixer, mix the potatoes and garlic on low speed just until smooth. Add the remaining ingredients and mix until smooth and fluffy. Serve hot.

(To make this recipe in advance, put in a 2-quart casserole and heat, covered, on low heat until ready for dinner.)

Tangy Zucchini Spears

Serves 6

This simple dish is a nice accompaniment to a menu including rich foods.

4 MEDIUM ZUCCHINI,
SLICED LENGTHWISE INTO
¼-INCH-THICK PIECES
1 CUP WHOLE-WHEAT
FLOUR
2 TABLESPOONS OLIVE OIL
3 CLOVES GARLIC, MINCED
2 TABLESPOONS RED WINE
VINEGAR
1 TEASPOON SALT
½ TEASPOON FRESHLY
GROUND BLACK PEPPER

Dredge the zucchini spears in the flour. In a large skillet, sauté the zucchini spears in the oil over medium heat for 5 minutes. Add the garlic and continue sautéing until tender. Stir in the vinegar and add the salt and pepper.

Savory Bread Pudding

Serves 6

This creamy pudding with a crispy crust is a wonderful holiday entrée. Serve it with Rich Mushroom Gravy (recipe follows) and it takes center stage for a traditional holiday dinner. I like to serve this in a large 2-quart casserole dish, but you can also use a 9-by-13-inch pan or even individual soufflé molds. For each serving, include some of the crusty top and the creamy center.

¼ CUP UNSALTED BUTTER, SOFTENED
6 SLICES WHOLE-WHEAT BREAD
½ TEASPOON DRIED SAGE
8 SCALLIONS, DICED
1 CUP CHOPPED PECANS
½ TEASPOON SALT
¼ TEASPOON FRESHLY GROUND BLACK PEPPER
4 CUPS MILK
4 EGGS

Preheat the oven to 350 degrees. Spray a 2-quart casserole dish with nonstick cooking spray. Butter the bread slices and cut into cubes. (You should have 4 cups bread cubes.) Place the cubes in the prepared dish and mix with the sage, scallions, pecans, salt, and pepper. In a small bowl, beat the milk and eggs together lightly. Pour the egg mixture over the bread cubes. Let soak for 20 minutes.

Bake for 45 minutes or until the pudding is firm when the dish is gently shaken. Serve immediately.

Rich Mushroom Gravy

Makes 3 1/2 cups

¼ OUNCE DRIED
MUSHROOMS
1 CUP BOILING WATER
1 MEDIUM ONION, DICED
3 CLOVES GARLIC, MINCED
2 TABLESPOONS UNSALTED
BUTTER
4 OUNCES FRESH MUSH-
ROOMS, CHOPPED
2 TABLESPOONS
UNBLEACHED FLOUR
½ TEASPOON PAPRIKA
¼ TEASPOON DRIED THYME
3 CUPS VEGETABLE BROTH
1 TEASPOON SALT
½ TEASPOON FRESHLY
GROUND BLACK PEPPER
1½ TEASPOONS BALSAMIC
VINEGAR OR TO TASTE

This gravy is a bit of work, but it is definitely worth it! A good sauce really makes a difference in a meal. I use a variety of dried mushrooms like shiitake, wood ears, and inexpensive Chilean mushrooms. This can be made ahead and reheated, as it does not get extremely thick.

Soak the dried mushrooms in the boiling water for 10 minutes. Sauté the onion and garlic in the butter over medium-high heat for 5 minutes. Add the fresh mushrooms and cook another 5 minutes or until the onion is translucent and the mushrooms are tender. Stir in the flour, paprika, and thyme. Slowly stir in the broth.

Strain the mushroom soaking liquid and set aside; mince the rehydrated mushrooms. Add the minced mushrooms and mushroom liquid to the gravy. Cook for 15 minutes or until slightly thickened. Add the salt, pepper, and balsamic vinegar. Serve hot.

Steamed Spinach

Serves 4 to 6

This is my favorite method of cooking greens. It is simple and fast and the quick cooking method retains the most spinach flavor. I sometimes add ½ cup sunflower seeds to this recipe.

1 (10-OUNCE) PACKAGE
   FRESH SPINACH LEAVES
3 CLOVES GARLIC, MINCED
2 TABLESPOONS EXTRA-
   VIRGIN OLIVE OIL

Wash the spinach well and drain lightly. In a nonstick skillet, sauté the garlic in the oil for 2 minutes over medium heat or until just fragrant. Stir in the spinach and cover and cook several minutes, stirring once or twice, until just wilted.

Cranberry-Orange Sauce

Makes 2 1/2 cups

1 (12-OUNCE) BAG
CRANBERRIES, FRESH
OR FROZEN
1 CUP FRESH ORANGE
JUICE (ABOUT 4
ORANGES)
½ CUP WATER
¾ CUP HONEY
2 TEASPOONS MINCED
ORANGE ZEST

This is my husband's favorite cranberry sauce and he insists that it be served at every holiday feast. You can also serve this fresh sauce as a filling for baked acorn squash or as an unusual ice-cream topping. You can vary this basic sauce by adding freshly grated ginger, chopped pears, chopped apples, or raisins.

Bring all the ingredients to a boil in a heavy saucepan and continue cooking over medium heat until the cranberries pop and the mixture becomes foamy. Cool, pour into a serving dish, and cover. Refrigerate until serving time.

Carrot Cake

Serves 15

This cake is a classic. Moist and rich, this is a nice addition to a holiday buffet. It also keeps well, so it can be made a few days in advance of a party or Christmas dinner.

2 CUPS SUGAR

2 CUPS WHOLE-WHEAT PASTRY FLOUR

2 TEASPOONS BAKING POWDER

1 TEASPOON SALT

2 TEASPOONS GROUND CINNAMON

1½ CUPS VEGETABLE OIL

4 EGGS

3 CUPS GRATED CARROTS

½ CUP CHOPPED WALNUTS

1 CUP RAISINS

Preheat the oven to 350 degrees. Spray a 9-by-13-inch baking pan with nonstick cooking spray. In a large bowl, whisk together the sugar, flour, baking powder, salt, and cinnamon. In a separate bowl, mix the oil and eggs until well beaten. Mix the dry ingredients with the wet ingredients and stir just until all the dry ingredients are incorporated. Fold in the carrots, walnuts, and raisins.

Pour the batter into the prepared pan. Bake for 35 to 40 minutes or until a toothpick inserted in the center comes out clean. Let cool on a wire rack and frost with Maple Cream Cheese Frosting (recipe follows).

Maple Cream Cheese Frosting

With an electric mixer, beat the cream cheese with the butter, maple syrup, and vanilla until smooth and light.

1 (8-OUNCE) PACKAGE CREAM CHEESE, SOFTENED

¼ CUP UNSALTED BUTTER, SOFTENED

⅓ CUP PURE MAPLE SYRUP

1 TEASPOON VANILLA EXTRACT

EGGNOG MANIA

1. I really like store-bought eggnog; you don't have to worry about using raw eggs and it is easy to jazz up. For traditional eggnog, add rum or bourbon to taste and always top with freshly grated nutmeg and substantial dollops of whipped cream.

2. Serve eggnog in a glass bowl surrounded by a larger bowl of ice. You can add diced bananas or pineapple to your traditional eggnog punch. Always chill glasses by putting them in the freezer at least 15 minutes before serving.

3. Substitute eggnog for milk in a custard pie. Or add a few tablespoonfuls to sour cream for an easy fresh-fruit dip.

4. Add chocolate syrup or cocoa to taste and serve either cold or warm for a new twist on eggnog.

5. Thaw frozen strawberries and puree with enough eggnog to make a thick breakfast shake.

6. Try frothing store-bought eggnog instead of milk to top espresso for a holiday cappuccino.

Eggnog Ice Cream

Makes 1 quart

Because chilling foods mellows the flavor, extra sugar and nutmeg are added to commercial dairy eggnog for this festive holiday ice cream.

2½ CUPS CHILLED DAIRY
  EGGNOG
⅓ CUP SUGAR
1½ TEASPOONS FRESHLY
GRATED NUTMEG

Mix the eggnog with the sugar and nutmeg until the sugar dissolves. Pour the eggnog mixture into an ice-cream maker and follow the manufacturer's instructions to freeze.

Easy Orange Shakes

Serves 8

I really enjoy this drink. I've included it with this menu for the children at the dinner, but obviously it is also wonderful with breakfast and brunch menus. To chill the glasses for this drink, simply rinse them in water and immediately put them in the freezer.

4 CUPS MILK, CHILLED
2 TABLESPOONS SUGAR
2 CUPS FRESH ORANGE
  JUICE, CHILLED
¼ TEASPOON ORANGE OIL
OR 1 TABLESPOON GRAT-
ED ORANGE ZEST

Pour all the ingredients into a blender and blend until frothy. Serve in chilled glasses.

GRACIOUS GIFTS AND PARTY FAVORS

1. One of my favorite ecological party favors is a tiny cedar or pine tree. Wrap the base in burlap and tie it up in red ribbon. Place a tree near each guest's plate. You can do the same thing with small herb plants.

2. A simple and easy hostess gift is to buy a holiday-themed oven mitt and fill it with a variety of wooden spoons, wooden pasta forks, and wooden spatulas. Tie the gift with a variety of ribbons and bells. Buy extra wooden kitchen utensils at this time of year and use them to decorate gifts and tuck into napkins for party favors.

3. If you can find child-size aprons, buy enough for your next children's party and personalize them with liquid paint. Use these for party favors as well as for holiday baking get-togethers with the kids.

4. A nice, inexpensive gift is to fill small brown paper bags with fireplace scents. Mix cinnamon sticks, pinecones, bay leaves, and large strips of orange peel in the bags and give them to guests to bring home and sprinkle on the logs in their fireplaces or use as potpourri.

5. Buy miniature wreaths and decorate them in a kitchen theme with tiny candy molds, cookie cutters, and other small tools glued to ribbons.

6. For a children's holiday party, use a colorful woolen scarf as a table runner. Tuck silverware into matching mittens and fill hats with small bags of candy or cookies.

7. I was at a holiday party once where the hostess put small bottles of gourmet spices, bubble bath, and condiments at each person's place setting. Personalized ornaments are also a nice party favor.

8. I like to buy a few extra holiday mugs each year. When you're in a bind and need a really quick holiday gift you can fill the mug with some homemade potpourri, Quick Trail Mix (page 191), or Spicy Garbanzo Nuts (page 196).

14

Gifts of Food

Butterscotch-Pecan Muffins

Painted Sugar Cookies

Spicy Gingerbread Men

Light Buttertop Wheat Bread

Mock Mincemeat

Quick Trail Mix

Easy Hermits

Herb Seasoning Mix

Herb and Spice Vinegar

Crock-Pot Apple Butter

Spicy Garbanzo Nuts

Buttery Pecan Toffee

Pickled Jalapeño Rings

Candied Citrus Peel

Savory Fresh Herb Butter

Chocolate-Covered Peanut Butter Balls

I've always thought homemade gifts are the best, and edible gifts are the best of all. I really enjoy giving a neighbor a homemade loaf of bread or baking a batch of Christmas cookies for my husband to take with him to work.

Butterscotch-Pecan Muffins

Makes 12 muffins

2 CUPS UNBLEACHED
FLOUR
½ CUP SUGAR
½ TEASPOON SALT
1 TABLESPOON BAKING
POWDER
1 CUP MILK
¼ CUP UNSALTED BUTTER,
MELTED AND COOLED
SLIGHTLY
2 EGGS
½ CUP CHOPPED PECANS
¾ CUP BUTTERSCOTCH
CHIPS

This recipe makes sweet, high-domed muffins that are perfect for either breakfast or brunch. Chocolate chips can be substituted for the butterscotch chips in this recipe. Muffins are generally best right after baking, but these will keep a day or so. Most muffins also freeze well and nothing is easier for a quick breakfast than reheating a frozen muffin in the microwave.

Spray a 12-cup muffin tin with nonstick cooking spray. Preheat the oven to 400 degrees. Whisk together the flour, sugar, salt, and baking powder. In a separate bowl, beat the milk, butter, and eggs together. Add to the dry mixture along with the pecans and butterscotch chips and fold together. Fill the muffin cups three-quarters full with batter. Bake for 18 to 20 minutes or until golden brown. Cool on a wire baking rack before serving.

Painted Sugar Cookies

Makes about 30 cookies

This is the basic sugar cookie dough I use. I really enjoy the pretty artwork you can do with these simple egg yolk paints. Use inexpensive children's paintbrushes for this recipe.

To make the cookies: In a large bowl, cream the butter and sugar. Add the egg, milk, vanilla, and orange oil. Sift together the flour, baking powder, and salt. Add the flour mixture to the creamed mixture. Wrap the dough in plastic wrap and refrigerate for 1 hour.

Preheat the oven to 375 degrees and spray a baking sheet with nonstick cooking spray.

To make the cookie paints: In each of 4 small cups, mix 1 egg yolk with ¼ teaspoon food coloring, one color for each cup.

On a floured surface, roll out the cookie dough to ⅛-inch thickness and cut with cookie cutters. Place the cookies on the prepared baking sheet and decorate with the paint. Bake for 8 to 10 minutes, until golden. Remove the cookies to a wire rack to cool.

Cookies

½ CUP UNSALTED BUTTER, SOFTENED
1 CUP SUGAR
1 EGG, BEATEN
¼ CUP MILK
½ TEASPOON VANILLA EXTRACT
2 DROPS ORANGE OIL OR 1 TEASPOON FINELY GRATED ORANGE ZEST
2 ¼ CUPS ALL-PURPOSE FLOUR
2 TEASPOONS BAKING POWDER
½ TEASPOON SALT

Cookie Paint

4 EGG YOLKS
¼ TEASPOON EACH RED, YELLOW, BLUE, AND GREEN FOOD COLORING

COOKIES AS ART

1. For some unusual name tags at your next dinner party, bake some fat gingerbread men and with white icing write each guest's name on a cookie. Or do sugar cookies in the shape of snowmen and paint on names with egg yolk paint.

2. Dress up bar cookies by piping ribbons and bows on each cookie to make it look like a tiny Christmas gift.

3. One of my favorite things to do with cookies is to make a wreath. Using gingerbread dough, make about ten 3-inch cookies all the same shape, such as maple leaves or chile peppers or holly sprigs. Then make a base out of a 12-inch circle of heavy cardboard and cut out a center circle about 8 inches wide. Glue on the cookies so they are overlapping and decorate as you please. You can coat the cookies with polyurethane to make a more permanent wreath.

4. Roll out basic sugar cookie dough onto a cookie sheet. Bake and decorate this large rectangular cookie with store-bought frosting. This is a truly unusual Christmas card for friends and family with a sweet tooth.

5. Add something fun to basic cookie doughs; use dried cherries or cranberries, diced dried apricots, grated citrus zest, currants, marshmallows, jelly beans, or butterscotch chips. Make your own colored sugars to sprinkle on cookies by tinting granulated sugar with a few drops of food coloring.

Spicy Gingerbread Men

Makes about 30 cookies

¼ CUP UNSALTED BUTTER, SOFTENED

½ CUP FIRMLY PACKED BROWN SUGAR

¾ CUP DARK MOLASSES

⅓ CUP WATER

3½ CUPS ALL-PURPOSE FLOUR

1 TEASPOON BAKING SODA

1 TEASPOON SALT

½ TEASPOON GROUND CINNAMON

½ TEASPOON GROUND GINGER

½ TEASPOON GROUND CLOVES

½ TEASPOON GROUND ALLSPICE

¼ CUP CURRANTS

These spicy cookies are terrific for holiday gift boxes as well as for decorating Christmas trees. If you're using these as Christmas ornaments, poke a hole through the top of each cookie with a drinking straw before baking and string with ribbon. This dough needs to be made several hours in advance or the night before you bake. All the messy work will already be done, so the kids can help the following day when it is time to cut out the cookies and bake.

In a large bowl, cream the butter and brown sugar. Add the molasses and water and beat until well blended. Sift the flour with the baking soda, salt, and spices. Add the flour mixture to the creamed mixture. Wrap the dough in plastic wrap and refrigerate 2 hours or overnight.

Preheat the oven to 350 degrees. Roll out the dough on a floured surface to ⅛-inch thickness and cut with cookie cutters. Decorate the cookies with the currants. Transfer to a greased baking sheet and bake for 10 to 15 minutes, until lightly browned. Remove the cookies to a wire rack to cool.

Light Buttertop Wheat Bread

Makes 2 loaves

I really started enjoying whole-wheat breads after I received a flour mill. Now I mill my own flour with hard red winter wheat berries from my natural foods co-op when I have time. If not, I purchase a high-quality whole-wheat flour. Both types of flour result in wonderfully light breads. Try several brands of whole-wheat flour before you give up on really light whole-wheat breads. They vary greatly in taste and quality. This bread is light and golden with a nice high rise. I like brushing butter on the top crust right after the bread has been removed from the oven to give it a little extra pizzazz. It is pretty enough to give for gifts and plain enough to be used for your regular daily bread.

¼ CUP HONEY
2¾ CUPS WARM MILK (ABOUT 110 DEGREES)
1 TABLESPOON ACTIVE DRY YEAST
4 CUPS WHOLE-WHEAT FLOUR, DIVIDED
1 TABLESPOON SALT
5 TABLESPOONS UNSALTED BUTTER, SOFTENED, DIVIDED
ABOUT 2½ CUPS BREAD FLOUR

Mix the honey, milk, and yeast and let dissolve 10 minutes in the bowl of an electric mixer. Add 3 cups of the whole-wheat flour and mix for 3 minutes on low speed. Cover with plastic wrap and let the sponge sit for 30 minutes. Add the salt, 3 tablespoons of the butter, the remaining 1 cup whole-wheat flour, and enough bread flour to form a stiff dough. Knead 10 minutes on low with the dough hook of the electric mixer. Form the dough into a ball and put in an oiled bowl, turning the dough to coat with oil. Cover with plastic wrap and let rise 1½ hours or until doubled. Punch down.

Spray two 4½-by-8½-inch loaf pans with nonstick cooking spray. Divide the dough into 2 pieces, form into balls, cover, and let rise for 45 minutes or until doubled. Bake in a preheated 375-degree oven for 45 minutes or until just golden brown. Immediately upon removing the loaves from the oven, remove them from the pans. Take the remaining 2 tablespoons of butter and rub it into the top of each loaf until it melts in. Let cool on a wire rack before slicing.

Mock Mincemeat

Makes about 4 cups

3 LARGE RED DELICIOUS APPLES, PEELED, CORED, AND DICED
½ CUP CHOPPED FIGS
½ CUP CHOPPED DATES
2 TABLESPOONS SUNFLOWER SEEDS
¼ CUP CHOPPED WALNUTS
¼ CUP HONEY
1 TEASPOON GROUND CINNAMON
¼ TEASPOON GROUND CLOVES
½ TEASPOON GROUND NUTMEG
½ TEASPOON GROUND GINGER

Put this vegetarian mincemeat in a pretty jar or crock and give it to friends and family members with a sweet tooth. It can be heated and served plain or can be used as an ice-cream topping or a stuffing for acorn squash. To make Mock Mincemeat Pie, prebake a pie shell until light golden and fill with one recipe Mock Mincemeat. Bake an additional 30 minutes at 350 degrees.

In a heavy saucepan, simmer all the ingredients over medium heat for 15 minutes, stirring occasionally. The mincemeat will keep, covered and refrigerated, for approximately 1 week.

Quick Trail Mix

Makes about 4 cups

This trail mix recipe is always an appreciated gift. Other ingredients (dried cherries, dates, sunflower seeds) can be added to taste. It can be presented in a jar or bottle or in a pretty dish tied up with a red ribbon.

½ CUP WHOLE ALMONDS
1 CUP RAISINS
1 CUP SEMISWEET CHOCO-
 LATE CHIPS
¾ CUP FLAKED COCONUT
½ CUP SUNFLOWER SEEDS
½ CUP UNSALTED PEANUTS

Mix together all the ingredients and store in an airtight container.

Easy Hermits

Makes 16 bars

These spicy bar cookies are quick and easy and store exceptionally well. In fact, they actually improve with age! Hermits are ideal for including in your Christmas cookie gift tins. Store them in an airtight container and they'll ship well to family and friends who are far away. I've also frozen these cookies with success.

½ CUP FIRMLY PACKED BROWN SUGAR
¼ CUP UNSALTED BUTTER, SOFTENED
1 EGG
½ CUP DARK MOLASSES
½ CUP BUTTERMILK
2 CUPS WHOLE-WHEAT PASTRY FLOUR
1 TEASPOON BAKING SODA
1 TEASPOON GROUND CINNAMON
1 TEASPOON GROUND NUTMEG
½ TEASPOON GROUND CLOVES
½ TEASPOON SALT
1 CUP RAISINS

Preheat the oven to 350 degrees. Spray an 8-inch square baking pan with nonstick cooking spray. With an electric mixer, cream the butter and brown sugar. Add the egg, molasses, and buttermilk and beat well. In a separate bowl, mix the flour with the baking soda, cinnamon, nutmeg, cloves, and salt. Mix the wet ingredients with the dry ingredients. Stir in the raisins. Spread the dough in the prepared pan and bake for 25 to 30 minutes or until the top is firm to the touch. Cut into 16 squares while still warm.

Herb Seasoning Mix

Makes about 2 tablespoons

This no-salt recipe is fun to make if you have a mortar and pestle. If you have any old spice bottles, fill them with this mixture and include some serving instructions when giving them to family and friends. This seasoning is tasty over baked potatoes, in bean soup, over brown rice, and with sweet potatoes.

Crush all the herbs and spices together well in a mortar and pestle or in a blender.

1 TEASPOON DRIED TAR-
  RAGON
1 TEASPOON DRIED
  OREGANO
2 TEASPOONS DRIED
  THYME
½ TEASPOON CELERY SEED
¼ TEASPOON FRESHLY
  GROUND BLACK PEPPER
½ TEASPOON PAPRIKA
½ TEASPOON DRY MUS-
  TARD
½ TEASPOON GARLIC
  POWDER
½ TEASPOON ONION POW-
  DER
¼ TEASPOON GROUND
  NUTMEG

Herb and Spice Vinegar

Makes 2 cups

2 CUPS RED WINE VINEGAR
3 SMALL DRIED CHILE PEP-
 PERS
3 CLOVES GARLIC, SLICED
2 (3-INCH) SPRIGS
 ITALIAN PARSLEY
1 TEASPOON BLACK PEP-
 PERCORNS
1 TEASPOON DILL SEED
1 TEASPOON MUSTARD
 SEED

This flavorful vinegar is a delightful seasoning for steamed vegetables. Kitchenware stores now stock a wonderful selection of colored and sculptured bottles that are perfect containers for flavored vinegars. Now that fresh herbs are available in stores year round, you can make herb vinegars anytime. If fresh parsley is not available, substitute dried herbs or other fresh herbs.

Bottle all the ingredients together and let sit for 2 weeks in a cool, dark place. Strain and use.

Crock-Pot Apple Butter

Makes about 7 1/2 cups

This recipe makes enough apple butter for several gifts, and the long, slow cooking guarantees a smooth, delicious butter. It keeps several weeks in the refrigerator and can also be frozen.

12 CUPS PEELED, CORED, AND SLICED TART GREEN APPLES, SUCH AS GRANNY SMITH
2 CUPS APPLE CIDER
1½ CUPS SUGAR OR TO TASTE
1 TEASPOON GROUND CINNAMON
½ TEASPOON GROUND ALLSPICE

Cook the apples and cider in a Crock-Pot, covered, for 12 hours on the low setting. Drain off any excess juice. Puree in batches in a food processor until smooth. Add the sugar, cinnamon, and allspice. Return the mixture to the Crock-Pot, cover, and cook on the low setting for 1 to 2 hours.

Spicy Garbanzo Nuts

Makes 2 cups

2 CUPS COOKED AND
DRAINED GARBANZO
BEANS
½ TEASPOON GARLIC POW-
DER
2 TEASPOONS CHILI POW-
DER

An unexpected bonus of making this recipe is the wonderful aroma that will fill your kitchen as the garbanzos bake. Don't drain the garbanzo beans too well, or the spices won't stick to the beans. Fill half-pint Mason jars with Spicy Garbanzo Nuts for gifts.

Mix the ingredients well on an ungreased nonstick baking sheet. Bake at 350 degrees for 45 minutes. Remove from the baking sheet to let cool.

Buttery Pecan Toffee

Makes 1 ½ pounds

This is one of my most requested holiday gifts. It takes a little more work, but it is very delicious and stores and ships well. You can substitute other nuts for the pecans. Almonds work well with this recipe, although they will need to be toasted first. I like to pour this toffee out onto my marble pastry board, but a greased cookie sheet will work also.

1¼ CUPS UNSALTED BUTTER

1 CUP SUGAR

¼ CUP FIRMLY PACKED LIGHT BROWN SUGAR

1 TABLESPOON HONEY

¼ CUP WATER

½ TEASPOON BAKING SODA

2 TEASPOONS VANILLA EXTRACT

1 CUP COARSELY CHOPPED PECANS

6 OUNCES SEMISWEET CHOCOLATE, FINELY CHOPPED

½ CUP FINELY CHOPPED PECANS

If using a cookie sheet, butter it well. In a heavy saucepan, melt the butter. Add the sugars, honey, and water and stir until the sugars dissolve. Cook over medium heat until the mixture reaches 290 degrees on a candy thermometer, stirring occasionally. Quickly stir in the baking soda, vanilla, and coarsely chopped pecans. Spread the mixture onto a marble slab or the prepared cookie sheet.

When the surface of the toffee is firm to the touch, sprinkle the chocolate evenly over the top. With a spatula, spread the melting chocolate completely over the surface. Sprinkle with the finely chopped pecans and let cool. Break into bite-size pieces to serve.

Pickled Jalapeño Rings

Makes 12 half-pints

5 POUNDS JALAPEÑO CHILE
PEPPERS
4 QUARTS PLUS 2 CUPS
WATER
1½ CUPS CANNING SALT
10 CUPS DISTILLED WHITE
VINEGAR
¼ CUP SUGAR
1 HEAD GARLIC, PEELED
AND SMASHED
1 MEDIUM WHITE ONION,
SLICED
2 TABLESPOONS WHOLE
BLACK PEPPERCORNS

The only two things I can regularly are peaches and these spicy chile peppers in brine. If you can't find jalapeños, substitute banana or Hungarian peppers. Decorate these jars with corn husk bows and whole dried chile peppers for unusual gifts. These peppers are good accompaniments to nachos, huevos rancheros, and chili. You'll need some canning supplies for this recipe: a large pot for processing the jars, several half-pint canning jars, and rubber gloves to protect your hands while slicing the jalapeños.

Rinse the jalapeños, slice into ¼-inch rings, and remove the seeds. Put into a large bowl with the 4 quarts water and the canning salt. Let sit for 12 to 24 hours. Rinse well and drain.

Make a pickling solution with the vinegar, sugar, and 2 cups water. Simmer this for 15 minutes and keep hot while canning. Pack the jalapeños in sterilized half-pint canning jars with equal amounts of the garlic, onion slices, and peppercorns. Fill the jars with the pickling solution, leaving ¼ inch of head space. Seal and process in a boiling water bath for 10 minutes. Refrigerate any jars that do not seal properly.

Candied Citrus Peel

Makes about 3 cups

Use any type of citrus peel you have available for this recipe: Orange, tangerine, lemon, lime, and grapefruit are all good. I recommend using organic fruit and washing the fruit well before peeling. After the peel is sugared, I sometimes melt some white and dark chocolate chips in the microwave and dip one-half of the pieces into the chocolate.

1 POUND CITRUS FRUIT
2½ CUPS SUGAR, DIVIDED

Rinse the fruit well. With a vegetable peeler, remove the peel in long strips from the fruit, keeping some of the white pith. Reserve the fruit segments for another use. Cut the peel into ¼-inch-wide strips.

Cover the peel with water in a heavy saucepan and bring to a boil. Discard the water and rinse well. Repeat this process twice to remove the bitterness. Add 2 cups of the sugar and ½ cup of water and stir well to dissolve the sugar. Cook for 45 minutes over medium heat or until the syrup evaporates, stirring occasionally.

Remove and cool the peel, separated, on wax paper. Put the remaining ½ cup sugar in a small shallow bowl. Dredge the cooled peel strips in sugar. Store in an airtight container.

Savory Fresh Herb Butter

Makes about ⅓ cup

⅓ CUP UNSALTED BUTTER,
  SOFTENED
3 SCALLIONS, FINELY
  DICED
1 TEASPOON FRESH LEMON
  JUICE
1 TEASPOON FINELY
  CHOPPED FRESH BASIL
1 TEASPOON FINELY
  CHOPPED FRESH THYME
2 TEASPOONS FINELY
  CHOPPED FRESH PARSLEY

Spoon this spread into a pretty crock or ceramic jar. It is a nice accompaniment to a homemade loaf of bread such as the Light Buttertop Wheat Bread (page 189). Use this butter to top baked potatoes, steamed mixed vegetables, pasta, or grains.

Mix all the ingredients together with a spoon and chill before serving.

Chocolate-Covered Peanut Butter Balls

Makes about 40 balls

My neighbor Cyn brought some chocolate peanut butter balls over to my house one day and I'm ashamed to admit I couldn't stop eating them! So I bugged her until she gave me her recipe. Since her coating recipe used paraffin, which may be hard to locate, I substituted a basic chocolate ganache coating. These confections are real kid-pleasers; Cyn makes them up in big batches and freezes them in Ziploc bags.

To make the peanut butter balls: Mix the peanut butter, cereal, butter, and confectioners' sugar. Cover and chill at least 2 hours. Roll into 1-inch balls and put on a cookie sheet lined with waxed paper. Chill for 2 additional hours.

To make the chocolate ganache coating: In a heavy saucepan, heat the cream and butter over medium-high heat. When the mixture comes to a boil, pour over the chocolate in a heatproof bowl and let stand for 5 minutes. Stir until smooth. Cool slightly.

To assemble, line 2 baking sheets with waxed paper. With a fork, dip each peanut butter ball in the chocolate ganache and cover thoroughly. Cool to room temperature, then chill until firm. Store in an airtight container.

Peanut Butter Balls

2 CUPS CREAMY NATURAL PEANUT BUTTER
2 CUPS CRISPY RICE CEREAL
½ CUP UNSALTED BUTTER, MELTED AND COOLED
2 CUPS CONFECTIONERS' SUGAR

Chocolate Ganache Coating

1 CUP HEAVY CREAM
2 TABLESPOONS UNSALTED BUTTER
12 OUNCES SEMISWEET CHOCOLATE, BROKEN INTO ½-OUNCE PIECES

HOW TO WRAP AND
SEND EDIBLE GIFTS

1. One of the most enjoyable parts about giving away edible gifts is the presentation. Give a big loaf of bread on a wooden pizza peel. Put quick breads in a pretty basket lined with red and green tea towels, pot holders, and oven mitts.

2. Cover canning jars and other bottles of goodies with fabric rounds tied with ribbon or lace.

3. One really nice hostess gift is what I call "the relaxation basket." Include all the necessities for an afternoon of pampering: some Chocolate-Mint Snowballs (page 108), a couple of boxes of herb tea, some bath salts and scented soaps, a risqué paperback novel, and a cassette tape of some relaxing music, such as light jazz.

4. To send food long distances, wrap it well. Bar cookies and drop cookies travel best and they should be wrapped individually in plastic wrap, then packed into a cookie tin.

15

Twelfth Night

HOME-STYLE
Supper

Raspberry Shrub

Creamy Zucchini-Corn Soup

Roasted Eggplant Salad

Marinated Herbed Carrots

Polenta with Chipotles and Sun-Dried Tomatoes

Cranberry-Nut Bread

Turtle Pie

Basic Piecrust

Consider wrapping up the holiday season with a Twelfth Night party. Twelfth Night is the night of January 5, the night before Twelfth Day, which is twelve days after Christmas. Twelfth Night is the official end to the Christmas season and is the final opportunity to host a holiday-related celebration.

This simple party fare can be made in advance to make your life easier. Take the time to pull your family together and critique the past holiday season. Did you do too much? What were your favorite events? What was your least favorite part of the holiday season? What can you do to make next Christmas even more fun and meaningful? This is the time to review the holiday and all you did.

This simple, homey menu is light on the waistline, which you'll probably appreciate after all those nights of bonbons and sparkling wine.

Raspberry Shrub

Serves 4

1½ CUPS FRESH OR
FROZEN RASPBERRIES,
THAWED
¼ CUP MILD APPLE CIDER
VINEGAR
¼ CUP SUGAR
2 TABLESPOONS CHOPPED
FRESH MINT
2 CUPS SPARKLING WATER,
SELTZER, OR CLUB SODA

This is a simplified version of a traditional American drink that is very refreshing before or after a meal. Use a mild type of mint, such as spearmint.

In a small dish, mix the raspberries with the vinegar and let stand for several hours or overnight. Puree the mixture in a blender or food processor. Add the sugar and mint and taste for sweetness. If too tart, add more sugar. (This mixture can be made in advance and refrigerated before serving.)

Mix ¼ cup of the raspberry mixture into ½ cup of sparkling water for each serving and serve over ice.

Creamy Zucchini-Corn Soup

Serves 4 to 6

This simple soup is easy to prepare with staples from the pantry.

1 LARGE ONION, DICED
2 TABLESPOONS UNSALTED
  BUTTER
4 CUPS SLICED ZUCCHINI
  (ABOUT 3 MEDIUM
  ZUCCHINI)
1 CUP VEGETABLE BROTH
1 (16-OUNCE) CAN
  CREAM-STYLE CORN
½ TEASPOON DRIED BASIL
SALT TO TASTE
2 CUPS MILK
CROUTONS OR SOUR
  CREAM, FOR GARNISH

Sauté the onion in the butter in a Dutch oven for 5 minutes or until transparent. Add the zucchini, stir well, and cook for an additional 3 minutes. Add the broth and simmer over medium-low heat, covered, for 20 to 30 minutes or until the zucchini is tender and most of the liquid is absorbed. Puree in batches.

Add the corn, basil, salt, and milk. Heat over low heat, stirring occasionally, until warmed through. Garnish with croutons or dollops of sour cream.

Roasted Eggplant Salad

Serves 6 to 8

1 EGGPLANT, PEELED AND
  CHOPPED
1 MEDIUM RED BELL PEP-
  PER, COARSELY CHOPPED
1 SMALL RED ONION,
  COARSELY CHOPPED
8 LARGE MUSHROOMS,
  QUARTERED
8 CLOVES GARLIC, HALVED
3 TABLESPOONS OLIVE OIL
1 TEASPOON SALT
FRESHLY GROUND BLACK
  PEPPER TO TASTE
3 TABLESPOONS BALSAMIC
  VINEGAR

This salad is a delicious addition to a large buffet dinner. It can be made in advance and can be served either warm or cold. Don't be alarmed at the amount of garlic used in this salad; it mellows considerably during roasting.

Preheat the oven to 450 degrees. In a baking pan, mix the eggplant, red bell pepper, onion, mushrooms, garlic, and oil. Bake for 20 to 25 minutes or until the vegetables are tender, stirring occasionally. Add the salt and pepper and toss with the balsamic vinegar. Chill and serve warm or cold.

Marinated Herbed Carrots

Serves 4

If you have fresh herbs available, substitute them for the dried tarragon in this dish. Chives and parsley work well in this recipe.

4 MEDIUM CARROTS, GRATED (ABOUT 2 CUPS)

2 TABLESPOONS FRESH LEMON JUICE

2 TABLESPOONS EXTRA-VIRGIN OLIVE OIL

1 TABLESPOON HONEY

1 TEASPOON DRIED TAR-RAGON OR 1 TABLESPOON FRESH

Mix all the ingredients together in a serving dish. Cover and chill for about 30 minutes for the flavors to blend.

Polenta with Chipotles and Sun-Dried Tomatoes

Serves 6

3 CUPS WATER

1 TEASPOON SALT

1 CUP POLENTA OR CORN-
MEAL

2 CLOVES GARLIC, MINCED

5 SUN-DRIED TOMATOES

1 DRIED CHIPOTLE CHILE
PEPPER

1 TABLESPOON UNSALTED
BUTTER

¼ CUP GRATED PARMESAN
CHEESE

¼ CUP GRATED SMOKED
CHEDDAR CHEESE

I make this recipe often; it is my favorite way to flavor polenta. I buy coarsely ground cornmeal, called polenta, at my health food co-op; regular cornmeal can be substituted if polenta is not available. Sun-dried tomatoes packed in oil and canned chipotle in adobo sauce can be substituted for the dried tomatoes and chipotle used in this recipe.

This needs to be made in advance. Use holiday cookie cutters to cut out interesting shapes for this fun dish.

Bring the water and salt to a boil over medium-high heat in a heavy saucepan. Pour the polenta in slowly, in a thin stream, stirring constantly. Add the garlic and cook the polenta until it starts pulling away from the sides of the pan, about 5 to 10 minutes.

Meanwhile, reconstitute the tomatoes and chipotle by pouring boiling water over both and let sit while the polenta cooks. After the polenta is fully cooked, mince the softened tomatoes and chipotle and add to the mixture. Stir in the butter and cheeses.

Sprinkle drops of cold water over a marble pastry board or a cookie sheet. With a firm spatula, spread the cooked polenta on the board to make a ¼-inch-thick rectangle. Let cool and cut into shapes with cookie cutters.

Place the shapes on a cookie sheet sprayed with nonstick cooking spray. Broil 4 inches from the heat source for 5 minutes and serve immediately.

Cranberry-Nut Bread

Makes 1 loaf

This pretty loaf is more tart than most and it keeps well. I like it served with Cranberry Butter (see page 162). To soften the cranberry butter, unwrap it and heat it in the microwave on High for 30 seconds.

2 CUPS UNBLEACHED FLOUR
¾ CUP SUGAR
1½ TEASPOONS BAKING POWDER
½ TEASPOON SALT
½ TEASPOON BAKING SODA
¼ CUP UNSALTED BUTTER, SOFTENED
¼ TEASPOON ORANGE OIL OR 1 TABLESPOON GRATED ORANGE ZEST
¾ CUP FRESH ORANGE JUICE
1 EGG
2 CUPS CHOPPED FRESH OR FROZEN CRANBERRIES
½ CUP CHOPPED WALNUTS

Preheat the oven to 350 degrees. Spray an 8½-by-4½-inch loaf pan with nonstick cooking spray. In a large bowl, whisk together the flour, sugar, baking powder, salt, and baking soda. Separately beat together the butter, orange oil, orange juice, and egg. Stir the wet ingredients and dry ingredients together until just mixed. Fold in the cranberries and walnuts. Pour into the prepared loaf pan and bake for 1 hour or until a toothpick inserted comes out clean. Let cool on a rack for 15 minutes before removing from the pan.

Turtle Pie

Serves 10 to 12

Caramel Layer
1 (14-OUNCE) PACKAGE
CARAMELS
⅓ CUP WHIPPING CREAM

1 RECIPE BASIC
PIE CRUST, BAKED AND
COOLED (RECIPE FOL-
LOWS)
1 CUP COARSELY CHOPPED
PECANS

Chocolate Topping
8 OUNCES SEMISWEET
BAKING CHOCOLATE, BRO-
KEN INTO ½-OUNCE
PIECES
⅓ CUP WHIPPING CREAM
¼ CUP CONFECTIONERS'
SUGAR

WHOLE PECANS, FOR GAR-
NISH (ABOUT 12)

I gave a few pieces of this pie to some neighbors and they were raving about it months later. Turtles are my favorite candy and this pie combines all the essentials: chocolate, pecans, and caramels. This pie is very easy to make using the microwave. (I think the hardest part about it is unwrapping all the caramels!) To make it even easier, use a prepared piecrust. For a simple garnish, you can put whole pecans around the edges of the pie. This pie is much easier to slice when it is at room temperature.

To make the caramel layer: In a microwave-safe dish, cook the caramels and whipping cream on High for 2 to 4 minutes, stopping every 30 seconds to stir, until the mixture is smooth and the caramels have melted. Stir well. Pour into the pie crust and top with the chopped pecans.

To make the chocolate topping: In a microwave-safe dish, cook the chocolate, cream, and confectioners' sugar for 2½ minutes or until the chocolate has melted and the mixture is smooth, stopping every 30 seconds to stir.

Pour the chocolate topping over the caramel layer, smoothing with a spatula. Garnish the top of the pie with whole pecans. Chill for 4 hours or overnight.

Basic Piecrust

Makes piecrust for 1 (9-inch) pie

Good piecrust takes a bit of work and advance planning, but it is worth every bit of the effort. First of all, I measure out the flour, salt, and sugar in the mixing bowl and chill the bowl and ingredients for at least 15 minutes. I also keep my vegetable shortening in the refrigerator so it will always be chilled. I like using a pastry blender for piecrusts, but forks or even a food processor can be used for mixing the crust. I've seen chefs on television use their hands, but I think the warmth of your hands can melt the fat in the crust. Do not overblend the ingredients. When adding the ice water, add just until the crust is starting to come together as a dough. If you have any dough left over after rolling out your crust, save the pieces and freeze them in plastic freezer bags. These "remnants" can be used for quick pastries or sugar cookies.

1½ CUPS UNBLEACHED
  FLOUR
1 TABLESPOON SUGAR
¾ TEASPOON SALT
¼ CUP CHILLED UNSALTED
  BUTTER, CUT INTO 1-INCH
  PIECES
¼ CUP CHILLED SOLID VEG-
  ETABLE SHORTENING
ABOUT ¼ CUP ICE WATER

Mix the flour, sugar, and salt in a bowl and chill. Use a pastry blender to mix in the butter and vegetable shortening until crumbly. Do not overblend.

Add the ice water, tablespoon by tablespoon, until the mixture just forms a ball. Wrap the dough in plastic wrap and chill 1 hour before rolling out.

Roll out to a 12-inch circle on a floured surface, flouring the rolling pin if the pastry sticks. Fold the pastry into quarters and gently transfer to a pie pan. Unfold and trim the edges of the piecrust as you wish. I like the easiest way of decorating piecrust, which is to use the tines of a fork to crimp the edges. Prick the bottom of the crust with a fork and bake at 400 degrees for 15 minutes, until golden brown. Cool completely before continuing with the recipe.

Christmas Resources

Here is some recommended reading on the subject of Christmas. Check your local library, bookstore, and video store for more holiday ideas and activities.

Celebrate the Bounty: Recipes and Rituals to Create Wonderful Feasts for Every Occasion in the Biblical Year, Amy Appleby and Jerald B. Stone, Ballantine/Epiphany, New York, 1990, ISBN 0-345-36129-6, paper, $8.95.

    This delightful book offers some excellent ways to celebrate biblical events, such as a Mexican Christmas dinner, a Christmas brunch, and an Advent dinner, along with recipes, offerings and graces, and biblical readings. All the foods in the recipes are either mentioned in or inspired by the Bible; a cookbook of body and soul.

Christmas: A Cook's Tour, Ingeborg Relph and Penny Stanway, Lion Publishing, Batavia, IL, 1991, ISBN 0-7234-0523-8, $25.95.

    This wonderful book offers Christmas recipes and customs from all over the world. Ikura in Nori Cones for the Japanese Christmas meal, Fried Flying Fish for the "Bajan Christmas Day Lunch," and Roast Turkey for the "Christmas Day Lunch in New England" are just a few of the tempting recipes and menus in this book.

Christmas from the Heart of the Home, Susan Branch, Little, Brown, New York, 1990, ISBN 0-316-10638-0, $19.95.

Not only is this book beautifully illustrated by the author, but it offers easy-to-follow, delicious recipes for your every Christmas need.

The Christmas Lover's Handbook: Or, How to Plan the Merriest Christmas Ever, Lasley F. Gober, Betterway Publications, Whitehall, VA, 1985, ISBN 0-932620-53-1, paper, $12.95.

This book may not still be in print, but it is worth searching for. Packed with holiday trivia, craft illustrations, party ideas, recipes, and gift suggestions, this encyclopedic paperback is a must for every Christmas lover's bookshelf.

Colette's Christmas: Cakes, Cookies, Pies, and Other Edible Art from the Author of Colette's Cakes, Colette Peters, Little, Brown, New York, 1993, ISBN 0-316-70206-3, $24.95.

This beautiful book is for the seasoned dessert maker and the dreamer. The designs in this book are showstoppers and it is worth the price alone for instructions for the Chocolate-Almond Pine Cones or the gorgeous Christmas Quilt Cake.

The Gingerbread Book, Steven Stellingwerf, Rizzoli International, New York, 1991, ISBN 0-8478-1414-9, $22.95.

This informative book offers complete instructions and photographs for making gingerbread masterpieces. From a gingerbread Christmas Sleigh to Hansel and Gretel's house, this book will help you become an accomplished gingerbread builder.

Home for the Holidays: Festive Baking with Whole Grains, Ken Haedrich, Bantam, New York, 1992, ISBN 0-553-07508-X, $25.

Ken Haedrich is the guru of whole-grain baking and this book is a compilation of all his favorite festive holiday recipes, including breads, Christmas cookies, cakes, pies, and even some savory baked dishes.

Martha Stewart's Christmas, Martha Stewart, Clarkson Potter, New York, 1989, ISBN 0-517-57647-3, $18.95.

Martha Stewart offers a wealth of decorating, cooking, and entertaining ideas in this beautiful book. Chapters on Christmas cookies, wreaths and topiaries, and gift baskets complement her holiday menus.

The Penny Whistle Christmas Party Book: Including Hanukkah, New Year's and Twelfth Night Family Parties, Meredith Brokaw and Annie Gilbar, Fireside/Simon & Schuster, New York, 1991, ISBN 0-671-73794-5, paper, $12.

This cheerful book is full of wonderful ideas, activities, and recipes for children's parties. Some of the ideas include a gingerbread log cabin, homemade menorahs, and a "Santa's Workshop" party.

Rose's Christmas Cookies, Rose Levy Berenbaum, Morrow, New York, 1990, ISBN 0-688-10136-3, $19.95

Every recipe I've tried from this delicious cookbook is wonderful. Ms. Berenbaum's recipes are very well tested and accurate and the photos are beautiful. Plus, she is the only baker I know with enough courage to attempt to make a gingerbread version of Notre Dame!

The Scented Christmas: Fragrant Decorations, Gifts and Cards for the Festive Season, Gail Duff, Rodale Press, Emmaus, PA, 1991, ISBN 0-87857-974-5, $17.95.

If you enjoy making homemade gifts, this well-written and -illustrated book offers many tasteful and elegant gift ideas using easy-to-find inexpensive materials. Imaginative crafts such as Christmas incense, old-fashioned pomanders, a Yule log, crackers, and Advent potpourri are included, as well as decorations and cards.

A Victorian Christmas – Joy to the World, Cynthia Hart and John Grossman, Workman, New York, 1990, ISBN 0-89480-825-7, $17.95.

This beautifully photographed book provides information on Victorian Christmas collectibles and customs. One of my favorite sections offers a Victorian Christmas list from a 1903 *Ladies' Home Journal.*

Mail-Order Sources

Casados Farms: Natural Foods from New Mexico, P.O. Box 1269, San Juan Pueblo, NM 87566.

Their small mail-order catalog offers a wide variety of dried chile peppers, as well as grains and spices.

The Chile Shop, 109 East Water Street, Santa Fe, NM 87501; (505) 983-6080; Fax: (505) 984-0737.

This catalog is the place to find all sorts of unusual chile peppers as well as some nice Southwestern dinnerware.

Community Kitchens, The Art of Foods Plaza, Ridgely, MD 21685; (800) 535-9901; Fax: (800) 321-7539.

Nice catalog of coffees and teas, as well as a variety of authentic New Orleans foods.

Gold Mine Natural Food Co, 3419 Hancock Street, San Diego, CA 92110-4307; (619) 296-8536; Fax: (619) 296-9756.

This catalog sells a lot of unusual grains and condiments, with an emphasis on macrobiotic and organic foods.

King Arthur Flour Baker's Catalogue, P.O. Box 876, Norwich, VT 05055-0876; (800) 827-6836; Fax: (800) 343-3002.

This catalog offers many baking supplies as well as books on the subject.

Sur La Table, 84 Pine Street, Pike Place Farmers' Market, Seattle, WA 98101; (800) 243-0852; Fax: (206) 682-1026.

Ask specifically for their baker's catalog; it includes a lot of unusual and elegant baker's supplies.

Sweet Celebrations, 7009 Washington Avenue South, Edina, MN 55439; (800) 328-6722; Fax: (612) 943-1688.

This is a catalog you'll really enjoy browsing through. Sweet Celebrations offers a good selection of cake, candy, and baking supplies.

Walnut Acres, Penns Creek, PA 17862; (800) 433-3998; Fax: (717) 837-1146.

Walnut Acres offers almost any natural food product you could ever want by mail.

Williams-Sonoma, Mail Order Department, P.O. Box 7456, San Francisco, CA 94120-7456; (800) 541-2233; Fax: (415) 421-5153.

This is a gourmet catalog with an attractive selection of dinnerware and kitchen appliances.

Index